GROWING TOGETHER

BOOKS
BY
ALAN S. BLINDER

GROWING TOGETHER

ALAN S. BLINDER

WHITTLE DIRECT BOOKS

The Larger Agenda Series is a registered trademark of Whittle Communications L.P.

Charts: Dale Glasgow
Photographs: John Maynard Keynes, Brown Brothers, page 3; Adam Smith, Brown Brothers, page 10; Paul Volcker, AP/Wide World, page 11; Richard Darman, AP/Wide World, page 12; George Mitchell, Robert Trippett/SIPA Press, page 29; Lester Thurow, courtesy of MIT News Office, page 46; Henry Ford, Brown Brothers, page 56; Marvin Runyon, Michael Clemmer/Picture Group, page 63.

Library of Congress Catalog Card Number: 91-65788
Blinder, Alan S.
Growing Together
ISBN 1-879736-01-2
ISSN 1046-364X

The Larger Agenda Series®

The Larger Agenda Series presents original short books by distinguished authors on subjects of importance to managers and policymakers in business and the public sector.

The series is edited and published by Whittle Books, a business unit of Whittle Communications L.P. A new book appears approximately every other month. The series reflects a broad spectrum of responsible opinions. In each book the opinions expressed are those of the author, not the publisher or the advertiser.

I welcome your comments on this unique endeavor.

William S. Rukeyser
Editor in Chief

CONTENTS

THE IDEA OF GROWTH

Times have changed. When Commodore Perry sailed into Tokyo Bay in 1853, he encountered a country that was, economically speaking, backward and inconsequential. The locals stood in awe of the military, technological, and economic power symbolized by Perry's "black ships." Military aspects aside, few Japanese feel that way today. Rather, it is Americans who blink in disbelief at the economic titan across the Pacific. Some hysteria accompanies this attitude, for Americans still enjoy a much higher standard of living than the Japanese. But no one doubts that the economic gap has narrowed drastically.

Here's a question: What growth rate in Japan produced this economic miracle? For reference, I'll supply a hint. Between 1870 and 1979, output per hour of work in the United States grew at a compound annual rate of 2.29 percent. Clearly, the corresponding Japanese growth rate was higher, or else they would not have closed the gap. But how much higher? Was it 6 percent? Or 5 percent? No, just 3.03 percent—a mere 0.74 percentage point higher than our own. That seemingly small growth differential, compounded for more than a century, transformed the relative positions of the two nations beyond recognition. Such are the wonders of compound interest.

And those wonders work in both directions. Looked at from across the Atlantic, we did to Great Britain more or less what Japan did to us. In about the same time-span, Britain slipped from being the world's preeminent economic power into the second rank of nations, while the United States rose to become the mightiest nation on earth. How did we pull off this feat? By growing a mere 0.51 percentage point per year faster in terms of output per hour, but maintaining that slim differential, on average, for more than a century. Yes, it takes a long time, but acorns really do grow into oak trees. And, relatively speaking, oak trees shrink back into acorns.

This short detour into economic history illustrates a simple but fundamental point: A small difference in a nation's economic growth rate, sustained for a long time, makes an enormous difference to the well-being of its people. Economic growth rates matter. Indeed, over a long enough time-frame, little else does.

Economic growth is a new idea in history. During the 16 centuries from ancient Rome to the dawn of the Industrial Revolution, humankind barely improved its material lot. But in the scant two centuries since then, and especially the last, the leading nations of the world have undergone a miraculous economic transformation. It is breathtaking to think that Americans of the mid-19th century had a life expectancy of only 40 years, that virtually none of them had indoor toilets, central heating or electricity, and that per capita output was roughly at the level of present-day Honduras. Breathtaking, but true.

Economic growth is not only a new idea; it is also a good idea. That there is virtue in enhancing people's material well-being hardly needs defense among economists. It is the raison d'être of an economic system, the main criterion by which we judge its success or failure. But growth is more than fried chicken, indoor plumbing, and cable TV. When the economic pie is expanding smartly, people have less need to quarrel over its division and can afford more charity toward their neighbors. Inventiveness is bountifully rewarded in a dynamic society, so technical and business innovations spread faster. When the economy booms, the government finds it easier to raise revenue for public purposes—whether those purposes be social welfare, support

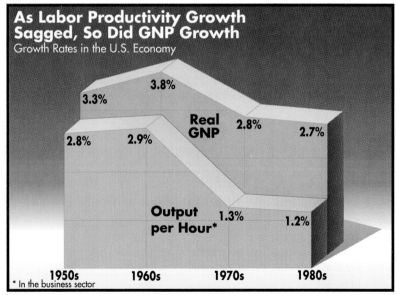

As Labor Productivity Growth Sagged, So Did GNP Growth
Growth Rates in the U.S. Economy

3.8%

3.3%

2.8%   2.9%   Real GNP   2.8%   2.7%

Output per Hour*   1.3%   1.2%

1950s   1960s   1970s   1980s
* In the business sector

Source: Economic Report of the President, 1991

for the arts, environmental preservation, or the ability to wage war. In short, economic growth makes more and more things affordable, and not all those things are material goods. Growth is enabling.

Unfortunately, this country's economic growth rate has lagged of late, as the accompanying chart shows. If we don't rev up the engine of economic growth, our country's future will be less bright than it could be, and our children and grandchildren will know exactly whom to blame. A 2.3 percent growth rate in real output per hour of work—which is about what we achieved during the century preceding 1980—if maintained for the next three decades, would leave output per hour 98 percent higher than it is today. A 1.2 percent growth rate—which is what we achieved in the 1980s—would leave it just 43 percent higher. There is much at stake in the growth game.

In recent U.S. history, there have been two periods in which the goal of faster growth captured the public imagination. John F. Kennedy riveted attention on growth in the early 1960s, and Ronald Reagan did it again in the early 1980s.

The growth strategy of the 1960s was, in the first instance, one of boosting spending. A quarter-century before, the economist John Maynard Keynes had taught the world a simple lesson: that more spending can lead to faster growth. But Kennedy was the first American president to apply this lesson deliberately. (It had, of course, often been applied inadvertently—such as in wars.) New Frontier economists devised a two-pronged growth strategy: First, use income tax reductions to stimulate consumer spending and get the U.S. economy producing up to capacity. Then use targeted investment incentives to speed the growth of capacity.

The economist John Maynard Keynes argued for increased government spending to reduce unemployment during the 1930s Depression.

The strategy worked wonderfully well—as far as it went. The Kennedy tax cuts did indeed get America moving again. But more spending is an inherently limited tool. Once full capacity is reached, which happened by about 1965, any further surge of demand is mainly dissipated in higher prices, not higher output—as the inflationary consequences of the Vietnam War painfully demonstrated.

Though its rhetoric was dramatically different, the Reaganomic growth strategy of the early 1980s was actually quite similar. The idea of using tax cuts to stimulate demand was not only disavowed but even denied by some of the zealots. It was, nonetheless, applied with a vengeance. Rhetorically, however, the central idea of Reaganomics was to prod the economy from the supply side. Actually, *unleash* is a better word than *prod*, for Reaganites refused to see the government as an active partner in the growth process. Rather, they insisted, the government should make way for the invisible hand of competitive markets by removing the visible foot of taxes and regulation. The Reagan program put special emphasis on strong tax incentives for saving and investment. The first seven letters of *capitalism* are, after all, *capital*. (One wonders if the reasoning went much deeper than that.)

Alas, the growth strategy of the 1980s encountered two small problems: it didn't work, and it left the American economy with a severe hangover. The failure of the Reaganomic growth strategy is the subject of chapters 2 and 3, where some aspects of the hangover will be detailed. The purpose is not recrimination, but rather to understand what we did, why we did it, and what went wrong. In brief, the bargain offered by supply-side economics was to trade greater inequality for faster growth. We got the inequality: by decade's end, the distribution of income in the United States was the most unequal of the postwar era. But the faster growth never materialized. Perhaps there was a flaw in the plan.

The premise of this book is that there must be a better way. There must be a way for the growth train to proceed without leaving the neediest at the station. I believe there is. Over the last five years or so, a variety of research findings from disparate sources has convinced me that there is an alternative strategy, ideally suited to the 1990s, that can promote growth without aggravating inequality. This strategy is outlined in chapters 4 through 6.

Before getting started, we should be clear about where the nation needs to go—and why. If faster growth is to be our goal, then growth in what? Gross national product grows faster if population grows faster. But that just makes our economy bigger, not better. It is better that we want. So growth must mean growth in output per person or per hour of work. But which?

Think for a moment about the difference. Output *per person* is the product of output *per hour* times the number of hours the average person works. But we call work *work* rather than *play* because it is often unpleasant; that's why we get paid to do it. So increases in output that come from toiling longer hours are at best a mixed blessing. History speaks with a clear voice on this point: over the centuries, as humankind has grown wealthier, people have devoted an increasing share of their time to leisure. So it makes sense to focus our attention on output per hour of work, that is, on the productivity of labor. It is slightly too simple, but only slightly, to say that standards of living advance in lockstep with labor productivity.

Thought of in this way, the 1980s emphasis on promoting capital formation seems a curiously roundabout means to the goal of higher living standards. I say roundabout, not wrongheaded, for the logic is impeccable. One way to make labor more productive is to equip workers with more and better capital. Doing so means investing more. So efforts in the 1980s to raise *labor* productivity by speeding the pace of *capital* accumulation were not misplaced. They were just indirect.

4

This book focuses on a more direct route: improving the quality of the labor force. The coming chapters spell out a growth agenda for the 1990s based not on capital formation but on developing the nation's *human* resources. It is a supply-side agenda, to be sure, but one aimed at bringing people together rather than pulling them apart. While it would almost certainly reduce inequality, it includes little in the way of overt redistribution. Finally, much as economists prize incentives and competition, the bywords of this program are *sharing* and *cooperation*. Yet incentives are not ignored.

The specific policy ideas on my menu are not new, though a few wrinkles are. My purpose is to bring a set of seemingly disparate ideas together into a coherent framework—a human-resource-based growth package for the 1990s that has a real chance for success. What are those ideas? Later chapters will flesh out the details and present the evidence supporting each. But to see where we are going, let me list the major ingredients here:

• Early intervention in the lives of children at risk to ensure that more of them grow up contributing to society rather than draining it.

• Various educational measures designed to improve the quality of the raw material that becomes our work force.

• More cooperative labor-management relations based on profit-sharing and employee involvement.

• Rebuilding our depleted stock of public-infrastructure capital such as roads, bridges, airports, and sewage-treatment facilities.

The last item calls attention to a conspicuous omission from my list: private capital formation—precisely the factor emphasized in the 1980s. It is not that I think private investment unimportant; far from it. But I do think we greatly overemphasized it in the growth strategy of the past decade, to the nation's detriment. Since this assertion flies in the face of conventional wisdom, I need to defend it. No one should support a radical change in direction if the old policies are working well. My contention is that they are not.

"What a beautiful night for flying."

Louis Turner
Pilot, Seattle

Our planes are equipped with Category III-A avionics, the most advanced in the industry. Which means that our pilots can land in weather when others can't. But more importantly, that we can deliver your shipments on time. When others might be late.

CHAPTER 2

THE LEGACY OF THE 1980s

The 1980s are gone, and some will say good riddance. It was a memorable decade for American capitalism, one epitomized by the good deeds of Michael Milken and Charles Keating and symbolized by Sherman McCoy's vanity and Gordon Gekko's greed. But above all the 1980s were the decade of Ronald Reagan. Rarely does a president put his stamp so firmly on America's society and economy; our system of government is dead set against it. But Ronald Reagan managed. Give him credit—and blame.

Chronological and economic time do not always correspond. In economic terms, the 1980s began on February 18, 1981, when the Reagan administration's fledgling economic team submitted a daring plan to Congress. Save for some details, we are still living the legacy of a strategy charted in *America's New Beginning: A Program for Economic Recovery*. In the space of just 26 pages, that notable document diagnosed America's economic ills (Jimmy Carter did everything wrong), posted clear goals for the 1980s (including faster growth with lower inflation), and provided a road map for getting there. About the diagnosis, I have nothing to say. (In the print media, you cannot roll your eyes.) With the goal of faster growth, I have already agreed enthusiastically. This chapter is about the road map and where it led us.

FOUR PREMISES

America's New Beginning bemoaned what it characterized as the stagnation of the recent past and projected a sharp acceleration of growth over the next five years—*if* the president's program was adopted. Critics labeled the forecast optimistic in the extreme; according to legend, a Ms. Rosy Scenario had worked it out in the White House basement. But administration spokesmen insisted that supply-side economics would belie the critics by reawakening the dormant spirit of enterprise.

This book argues that the premises underlying the Reaganomic growth strategy were fundamentally flawed, making failure entirely predictable. Indeed, the alternative program offered here is predicated on ideas that are virtually the opposite of those underpinning the Reagan program. It seems imperative, therefore, to start by clearly enunciating the Reaganite premises. Four seem most central:

1. *Government is an obstacle to growth.* "More government intervention in the economy cannot possibly be a solution to our economic problems," the report asserted on its opening page. Soon the dictum that government is part of the problem, not part of the solution, became a White House mantra. What we needed to do, the new administration insisted, was remove barriers to private entrepreneurship "by reducing the burdensome, intrusive role of the Federal Government; by lowering tax rates and cutting spending; and by providing incentives for individuals to work, to save, and to invest." In stark contrast, this book argues that a government seriously interested in promoting growth has much to do—other than just getting out of the way.

2. *Lower taxes are the route to improved incentives.* Belief in the power of incentives is the economist's equivalent of a union card; it almost defines our trade. But Reaganomics naively equated better incentives with lower marginal tax rates, as if the two were one and the same. "The tax system has been a key cause of our stagnation," the report claimed. "Personal tax reductions will allow people to keep more of what they earn, providing increased incentives for work and saving. Business tax reductions will provide increased incentives for capital expansion, resulting in increased productivity for workers." Improved incentives play an essential role in the growth program propounded in this book. But they take forms other than tax cuts.

3. *Private capital formation is the key to growth.* The third premise is found in the closing words of the previous quotation: More rapid capital accumulation—achieved through tax breaks for savers and investors—should be the main engine of productivity growth. Of all the claims made by the Reagan team, this one encountered the least criticism, for it was—and is—most in accord with conventional wisdom. At one level, of course, the premise is too simple not to be true. Who doubts that you can raise labor's productivity by equipping each worker with more and better capital? The hard part comes in arguing that capital formation is the superhighway to productivity improvement and that tax incentives are the entrance ramp. The next chapter will argue that, in fact, they are not.

4. *America needs cowboy capitalism.* The fourth premise of Reaganomics was not apparent in *America's New Beginning*—unless you were awfully good at reading between the lines. It was, instead, an unstated and unsavory corollary that became clear only as the decade unfolded. In his motto, "greed is good," Gordon Gekko, the fictionalized Ivan

Boesky of the film *Wall Street*, put crudely what Adam Smith had phrased more finely in 1776: "[A businessman] neither intends to promote the public interest, nor knows how much he is promoting it . . . he intends only his own gain, and he is . . . led by an invisible hand to promote an end which was no part of his intention."

This message, of course, has been part of Western economic thought for two centuries. It is one of history's great ideas. But it is too simple in several important respects. Over the centuries, capitalist societies have therefore tempered the invisible hand in many ways: with progressive taxation and social-welfare programs, with environmental and consumer protection, with antitrust enforcement, and so on. American capitalism in the 1980s was a throwback to an earlier, intemperate capitalism. Make a buck. Make it now. Leverage to the hilt. Trade companies like baseball cards. It was cowboy capitalism: come in with six-guns blazing, win the day, and move on.

Taken together, these four premises posed a troubling question that the American public barely paused to ask in the heady days of 1981. If we clear the deck for economic Darwinism, what will become of the unfit? The Reagan administration had two answers. One was the vaunted social safety net, which it promptly tattered. The other was the notion that the free-flowing benefits of renascent capitalism would trickle down to even the lowest reaches of society. A rising tide raises all boats, enthusiasts enthused. But skeptics wondered if the wake of a big ocean liner might not flood a leaky rowboat.

The Scotsman Adam Smith, founder of modern economics, frowned on government interference, confident that self-interest would lead to public gain.

THE DISPROOF OF THE PUDDING

What of the results? Did Reaganomics deliver? This question is still being debated, and I may not be an impartial arbiter. But facts are facts and, at least to some extent, speak for themselves. Let me begin with the achievements of Reaganomics, for there surely were some.

Most important was the long, uninterrupted economic expansion that began as winter dawned in 1982 and lasted until the summer of 1990. Rarely in U.S. history have expansions lasted so long. And this one carried the civilian unemployment rate all the way down to 5.1 percent, a rate not seen in this country since 1974. Indeed, in the late 1970s and early 1980s, many of my fellow economists had reached the doleful conclusion that an unemployment rate somewhere between 6 and 7 percent was the lowest the U.S. economy could sustain. I never believed that, and the Reagan boom proved the doomsayers wrong. Much more important, it provided jobs for millions. Though other factors must share the credit, the Reagan tax cuts helped power the expansion. It was a notable achievement.

Reaganomics is often also credited with breaking the back of inflation. That is hardly surprising; presidents are routinely given blame and credit for all manner of things beyond their control. And the fact is that inflation did fall dramatically on Ronald Reagan's watch. But a careful examination of the facts stubbornly assigns the credit elsewhere.

Fact: Inflation was dropping rapidly before President Reagan's inauguration. The Consumer Price Index rose at a 16 percent rate in the first half of 1980 but only at a 9 percent rate in the second half. Not even the Teflon president could influence the past.

Fact: Nothing in the 1981 economic program—other than exhortations to the Fed to maintain its tight-fisted policy—can remotely be called anti-inflationary in the short run. Yet inflation fell *immediately.* Tight money, not supply-side tax cuts, killed inflation.

Fact: It is disingenuous to claim credit for slaying the inflationary dragon while simultaneously avoiding blame for the 1981–1982 recession, as partisans of Reaganomics still try to do. This revisionist interpretation of history simply won't wash. The fact is that recession is the medicine that cures inflation. If Paul Volcker bears the onus for the slump, he also deserves the kudos for defeating inflation.

A third achievement, much prized by Mr. Reagan and his supporters, is more legitimate. Supply-siders focused single-mindedly on lowering marginal tax rates. And lower them they did. When Ronald Reagan came into office, personal income tax rates went as high as 70 percent in the upper-income brackets. When he left, no one paid more than a 33 percent marginal rate, and top earners paid just 28 percent.

Paul Volcker, chairman of the Federal Reserve Board from 1979 to 1987, fought inflation with tight money, which triggered the worst economic downturn since the Depression.

The likely benefits of tax-rate reductions were, of course, wildly exaggerated by the administration. Charles Schultze, then a Carter economic adviser, got it right when he quipped that there is nothing wrong with supply-side economics that division by 10 couldn't cure. But even dividing by 10 leaves some benefits. Lower tax rates do provide greater incentives to work, to save, and to invest—and weaker incentives to avoid taxes. A cleaner tax code with lower rates and fewer loopholes had long been a cherished goal of liberal tax reformers. That it remained for the most conservative president since Calvin Coolidge to make it a reality was ironic, but most welcome.

But what about the subject of this book—speeding the pace of economic growth? Did supply-side economics work? I'm afraid not. During the five years ending in 1981, the U.S. economy grew by an average of 2.9 percent per year—a rate the Reaganites derided as grossly inadequate. Over the next five years, however, the growth rate slipped a notch to 2.7 percent.

Supply-siders will object that five years is too short a time-frame to judge by. Agreed. The nine years from 1981 to 1990 is the longest period we can now use to appraise the Reagan economy. Calling the

1981-1990 period the 1980s for short, and using the preceding nine years as the 1970s, the score tilts slightly in Reaganomics' favor: growth averaged 2.8 percent in the 1980s versus 2.5 percent in the 1970s. But when the dust settles on the current recession and we add a 10th year to the data, the edge will probably shift back to the pre-Reagan period. The point is that no honest reading of the data can detect any sizable acceleration of economic growth.

If we focus more narrowly on productivity in the private business sector, a slightly better case can be made for Reaganomics, though it is a thin one. Output per hour of work increased at an average annual rate of 1.2 percent in the 1980s versus only 0.9 percent in the 1970s. Both are remarkably poor performances, to be sure. An increase in the productivity growth rate of three-tenths of a percentage point hardly qualifies as a rebirth of capitalism. But 1.2 percent is better than 0.9 percent, no doubt.

Finally, what about saving and investment, the Reaganites' favorite engines of growth? The saving part of this question is easily answered: supply-side economics was a flop. Despite tax incentives galore and sky-high real interest rates, American households actually saved a smaller share of their after-tax incomes in the 1980s than they did in the 1970s. The extent of the decline is really quite remarkable. Personal saving per capita was actually 23 percent lower in inflation-corrected dollars in 1990 than it had been a decade earlier, despite substantial economic growth in the interim. In fact, while real incomes have risen about 50 percent since the late 1960s, the average American family today saves no more in inflation-corrected dollars than its counterpart did almost a generation ago.

Richard Darman, a key figure in the Reagan Treasury, shepherded tax reforms through Congress during 1986.

Economists will tell you, correctly, that personal saving is only part of the story. To get a proper picture of *national* saving, you must add business saving and subtract the government budget deficit. Doing so, however, makes the comparison even less favorable to Reaganomics. America as a nation saved an average of 16.8 percent of GNP in the decade before Ronald Reagan became president, but only 13.7 percent since. This insouciance about the future, I suppose, is what Richard Darman calls now-nowism. It neatly encapsulates the spirit of the age.

The investment picture is cloudier, for it depends critically on one of those boring accounting issues: whether you measure capital on a gross or net basis. (The difference is depreciation.) Data on gross investment score Reaganomics a modest success. As a share of gross national product, gross business fixed investment averaged 12 percent over 1981-1990 versus 11.2 percent in the previous decade. A rise of eight-tenths of a percentage point hardly constitutes a capitalist revolution, but it does at least go in the right direction. Unfortunately, data on net business fixed investment tell the opposite story: it declined from 3.6 percent of net national product to 2.8 percent.

This ambiguity in the data allows both proponents and detractors of Reaganomics to have fun with numbers. Thus one economist can tell you that investment rose in the 1980s while another assures you that it fell. Both are right by their own definitions. But, as a gesture of goodwill, let's score this one in favor of Reaganomics. Say that supply-side economics stimulated investment slightly. (*Slightly* is, in all honesty, the best we can say.)

If saving fell sharply as a share of GNP while investment rose a bit, two obvious questions arise. First, with more firms scrambling for funds and fewer funds available, shouldn't interest rates have risen? Indeed, they did. Real interest rates soared in the 1980s to levels not seen in the United States in a half-century.

Second, if Americans were saving less, who was financing all that investment? The answer, of course, is that we borrowed the money from bankers in Tokyo, burghers in Frankfurt, gnomes in Zurich, and anyone else in the world who would lend it. The United States of America became a giant financial vacuum cleaner sucking in money from around the globe. In consequence, we are now in hock up to our ears. That, too, is part of the legacy of Reaganomics.

In fact, much of the unwanted inheritance of the 1980s can be summarized in what is fast becoming the four-letter word of the 1990s: debt. America as a nation now owes a whopping debt to foreigners. Our national government has accumulated a debt that was unimaginable in 1980. Our savings and loan industry has imploded, leaving in its wake a crater of debt big enough to swallow the FSLIC, the reputation of Congress, and an unbelievable amount of the taxpayers' cash. An unseemly number of American corporations owe obscene sums to banks, bondholders, and even less well-secured creditors. And the banks themselves sit sheepishly atop a mountain of bad loans that threatens their very survival.

The cartoonists, as usual, have captured the moment poignantly. In one cartoon, a bank's loan officer hands a check to a borrower with the droll admonition, "Don't try to cash it 'til Thursday." In another, a department-store salesman offers his customers "a free bank with every toaster you purchase."

All this would be funny if it weren't deadly serious. America will spend most of the 1990s recovering from the debt hangover of the 1980s. Already, bankruptcy is becoming the specialty of choice of our ever-adaptable legal profession. And the same folks who earned handsome fees arranging hostile takeovers and leveraged buyouts are now earning handsome fees peddling financial restructurings, debt workouts, and prepackaged bankruptcies. The

"I can make a BMW go faster."

Friedrich Winther
Freight Handler, Dingolfing, W. Germany

By using Federal Express® to fly BMW parts to the U.S. directly from Germany, BMW
dealers can make customers' cars fly out of the shop in just days.

1980s were a period of cowboy capitalism, all right. But unfortunately, the nation got *Maverick* instead of *Wagon Train*.

THE SQUEEZE ON THE LOWER 80 PERCENT

There is yet another part of the legacy, perhaps even more troubling than the first. The 1980s witnessed a redistribution of income and wealth on a grand scale—far greater than in Lyndon Johnson's Great Society and perhaps comparable to Franklin Roosevelt's New Deal. But there was a striking difference this time: the wealthy were on the receiving, not the giving, end. Social policy oozed sympathy for struggling Wall Street yuppies scraping by on $600,000 a year while the administration explained that ketchup is a fine vegetable for the poor.

The old song line "the rich get rich and the poor get poorer" used to be a gross misreading of American history. From the depths of the Great Depression until some time in the 1970s, high- and low-income families grew more prosperous together in America, with the poor gaining slightly on the rich. Income gaps narrowed, though at a glacial pace. Then everything began to change at once. Income growth slowed and inequalities began to widen. The old song began to ring true.

In fairness, both of these reversals predated Reaganomics and cannot be attributed to it. From 1973 to 1989, average family income advanced only about 1 percent a year in inflation-corrected dollars versus nearly 3 percent a year from 1947 to 1973. But families near the top escaped most of the slowdown and continued to prosper. During the 16 years ending in 1989, the real income of the average American family grew just 16 percent. But the richest fifth managed real income gains of 26 percent, and the top 5 percent saw their incomes rise 34 percent.

The law of averages holds a nasty implication: if the top 20 percent of income recipients do much better than average, the lower 80 percent must do worse. They did. And the news deteriorates as you near the bottom of the income ladder. The poorest fifth of families lost out not just relatively but absolutely. Their real incomes fell almost 4 percent. It's an odd sort of world in which 80 percent of the people do worse than average, but that's the way it was in the late 1970s and throughout the 1980s. If it was morning in America, someone forgot to awaken most of our citizens.

The U.S. Bureau of the Census has kept the data on income distribution since 1947. In all this recorded history, 1989 stands out as the year with the most unequal income distribution of all. The accompanying chart shows what happened in the 1980s by comparing the shares of total income received by the poor and the rich at the start and end of the decade. The year 1973 is included to show that the trend toward greater inequality proceeded at a snail's pace between 1973 and 1979 even though income growth slowed markedly. The rich are defined as the top 5 percent, the poor are the lowest 20 percent, and the middle class (not charted) is everyone in between.

The conclusion is clear: The rich gained on everyone else. In 1979, the income of a typical family in the top 5 percent was 12 times that of a typical family in the bottom 20 percent. By 1989, this ratio had risen to almost 16. Such nameless, faceless statistics paint a grim picture of a society pulling apart at the extremes, separate and unequal, not bound together by a common economic fate. The 1980s were a wonderful decade to be rich. For the rest, it was not so hot.

To most of us, life in the bottom 20 percent of the income distribution (family incomes below $16,000 in 1989) is something to be read about in newspapers and magazines, not to be experienced firsthand. It is a world of broken families and teenage mothers, of illiteracy and unemployment, of drugs, disease, and street crime that make life expectancy in Harlem no better than in Bangladesh. In the late 1970s and 1980s, those with the least to lose lost the most. Three main factors contributed to their travails.

The first is that the government lowered the social safety net peril-

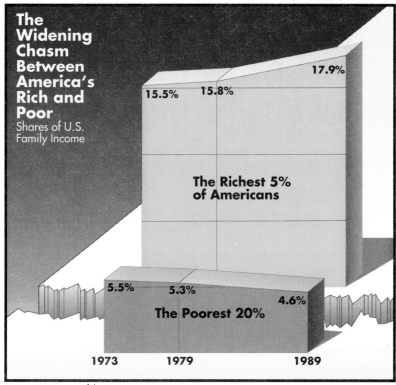

The Widening Chasm Between America's Rich and Poor
Shares of U.S. Family Income

15.5% 15.8% 17.9%

The Richest 5% of Americans

5.5% 5.3% 4.6%
The Poorest 20%

1973 1979 1989

Source: U.S. Bureau of the Census

ously close to the floor. Families in the bottom fifth of the income distribution rely on welfare for just over half their daily bread, and Aid to Families with Dependent Children and food-stamp benefits declined about 30 percent after inflation between 1972 and 1988. (Note, once again, that the trend predated Ronald Reagan.)

The second reason is obvious—and germane to the theme of this book: the poor own little capital and so were in no position to benefit from a growth strategy that emphasized tax incentives for saving and investment. In 1980, the U.S. economy generated 22 cents of interest and dividend income for every $1 of labor income; by 1990, that figure had climbed to 27 cents. Needless to say, it was not the people at the bottom who collected the additional pennies.

Finally, even trickle-down economics holds little hope for people who derive only about 35 percent of their income from earnings; the other 65 percent is immune to any upward pull on wages.

Where did the real winners of the 1980s live? At the top of the income distribution, of course. A typical family in the richest 1 percent had a total income in 1990 of about $550,000, of which $260,000 came from earnings and $280,000 from interest, dividends, and capital gains. Not bad. Such families were ideally situated to benefit from both tax incentives for saving and investment and from the high interest rates that prevailed. That capital income grew about three times as fast as labor income in the 1980s (after correcting for inflation) suited these families just fine. After all, they owned the capital.

The top 1 percent is atypical, almost by definition. Most high-income people derive the lion's share of their income from work. Among the richest 20 percent of families, for example, some 72 percent of all income comes from labor; just 23 percent comes from capital. Still, 23 percent is not nothing, and these people did benefit from the tax breaks of Reaganomics.

But there was a much more powerful force at work, one not attributable to Reaganomics—at least I don't think so. During this period, the distribution of wage rates grew substantially more unequal. In terms of purchasing power, wages at the bottom fell while wages at the top rose.

The reasons behind this widening of the wage distribution are not well understood, but the facts are stark. Between 1979 and 1989, the median income of male college graduates rose about 5 percent more than inflation, while high-school graduates lost more than 16 percent, and high-school dropouts fared even worse. The income gap between high-school and college graduates, which had narrowed slightly during the 1970s, widened dramatically during the 1980s. Among males, the median income of college graduates was 39 percent above that of high-school graduates in 1979, but 73 percent above in 1989. (For females the corresponding figures were 86 percent and 107 percent.) It was a good decade to be a lawyer, an engineer, or a stockbroker and a bad decade to work on an assembly line.

This same fact emerges almost any way you slice the data. Wages near the top of the distribution rose faster than wages near the bottom. Salaries of CEOs rose rapidly in real terms while the purchasing power of the minimum wage fell. Wages of skilled workers rose faster than those of the unskilled. Earning rates in high-paying industries rose faster than those in low-paying industries. Wages of experienced workers grew much faster than entry-level wages. Even within narrowly defined demographic groups (say, white men age 25 to 34 with a high-school diploma), the distribution of earnings spread out. It was the age of inequality.

It is this last factor—the widening inequality of wages—that accounts most for the squeeze on the middle class. The middle 60 percent of the income distribution derives about three-quarters of its income from wages and salaries, less than 10 percent from interest and dividends. And these people do not take home the highest wages, but those nearer the middle. When middle-class wages sag, middle-class family incomes do too. That is precisely what happened in the 1980s. And it should not necessarily be blamed on Reaganomics.

It is by now well known, though vigorously disputed by the Reaganites, that these factors were exacerbated by the 1981–1984 tax cuts, which were heavily skewed toward the rich. According to estimates by the Congressional Budget Office, the overall federal tax burden hardly changed between 1977 and 1990; but the distribution of the burden did. In particular, the richest 1 percent got a large tax cut, the next 4 percent got a small tax cut, and everyone else got an increase. If that's not a tilt toward the rich, I don't know what is.

You get a quite different impression, however, by listening to proponents of Reaganomics. They point out, correctly, that the top 1 percent of families paid 15.7 percent of all federal taxes in 1990 versus only 13.6 percent in 1977. How then, they ask, can anyone claim that the tax cuts of the 1980s were skewed toward the wealthy?

Simple. First, some of the disequalization was reversed by the 1986 tax reform; it was only the tax cuts of the first Reagan term that enriched the rich. Second, if the very rich were increasing their slice of the economic pie, as they were during the 1980s, an unchanged tax law would have automatically increased their share of total taxes paid. If the tax law tilted in their favor, their share of taxes would have risen less than their share of pretax income—which is precisely what happened. Between 1977 and 1990, the richest 1 percent of families increased their share of pretax income by a whopping 53 percent but increased their share of taxes paid by only 15 percent.

What the data add up to is this: For whatever reasons, our market economy began in the late 1970s to dish out relatively more handsome rewards to the well-off and relatively niggardly ones to the working classes. Not all of this can be attributed to Reaganomics—perhaps not most. But Reaganomics compounded the problem by diminishing the welfare state, slashing the tax burdens of the wealthy, and, in conjunction with the Federal Reserve's tight monetary policy, pushing real interest rates into the financial stratosphere. Thus the market and the government worked in concert to produce the greatest disequalization of incomes that U.S. economic history has ever seen.

CHANGING DIRECTION

Economic growth should not be a spectator sport. A nation cannot truly progress if it leaves 80 percent of its people behind, and a democratic nation should not want to. The growth policy of the 1980s served the interests of the wealthy wonderfully well. But only a trickle trickled down. What we need in the 1990s is a growth policy that works better for the majority—a policy that, in Lincoln's ringing phrase, is designed "for the people."

The search for such a policy is not founded on the politics of envy, as conservative critics claim. It is based on the politics of inclusion—the only valid politics in a democratic society. Nor need such a growth policy emphasize confiscation of wealth, or even much overt redistribution. Yes, the lower 80 percent was the aggrieved party of the 1980s. But much of their plight had nothing to do with government policy, and none of it will be solved by class warfare.

What is needed in the 1990s, I believe, is a growth policy that focuses on shoring up the middle and lower classes and from which the rich can benefit too—by what might be called percolate up. It is my contention that such a policy can be built on a human-resource base.

And there is one more critical ingredient. A growth policy for the 1990s must not be premised on pie in the sky; we had enough of that in the 1980s. Those who promise miracles are, more often than not, selling elixirs. We must base our new growth strategy on facts, not hopes; on logical reasoning, not wishful thinking; on evidence, not slogans. All this was sorely lacking in the 1980s, when caution was thrown to the wind and policies were adopted on faith.

CAPITAL OFFENSES

I f you are a reading person, you have certainly encountered the case for capital formation: Tax incentives boost investment and that, in turn, spurs growth. Growth is good, and therefore so are tax incentives. End of case. The message is so eloquently simple, and by now has been repeated so many times with such authority, that it may appear eccentric or even boorish to dispute it. Nonetheless, that is precisely what I propose to do.

There is no percentage picking on a platitude. But my target is far less sacrosanct than the conventional wisdom would have us believe. Stripped to its essentials, the case for providing tax incentives for capital formation consists of four logical elements. First, one way to raise labor productivity is to equip each worker with more and better capital. No quarrel there. Second, the best way to get more investment is to proffer tax inducements for individuals and businesses to save and invest more.

Here the argument often ends, conveniently omitting its weakest points. In fact, however, there are two more crucial, often unstated, and quite dubious items in the illogic. Item three is the assertion that the government (or the editorial board of *The Wall Street Journal*) knows how to design tax incentives that really work. Item four is the presumption that these incentives have minimal or no negative side effects.

This chapter takes issue with the last three items in the argument, and especially the final two. I will argue that designing effective tax incentives is much harder than it appears, that most incentives have significant adverse side effects, and—most fundamentally—that there are better ways to do the job.

Let me be clear at the outset. This is not a brief against capital formation. If Americans woke up tomorrow with a newfound desire to save and invest more than ever before, I would lead the cheering. But stating that the commonweal is well served by providing tax incentives to do so is another thing entirely.

GIMME SHELTER

The how-to manual for tax incentives is based on a disarmingly simple precept: jigger the tax code so that those who invest can make a
bundle. Those four words—*jigger the tax code*—are music to the ears
of lawyers and accountants. Play it and you may be amazed by the
display of creative energy that suddenly springs to life. In the art of
tax avoidance, the early 1980s were the Renaissance, and the tax-
writing committees of the House and Senate were the Medici.

Simple ideas are sometimes complicated in the execution, however. The details of tax incentives for investment certainly are. Worse
yet, they are the stuff that makes accountants' hearts beat faster and
puts everyone else to sleep. Mindful of the quip that economists are
people who lacked the personality to become accountants, I will deal
briefly with only four tax breaks.

Tax Break #1: To President Reagan's incoming team in 1981, accelerated depreciation was the Mona Lisa of investment incentives.
Though it is a very old idea (having been introduced to the tax code
in 1954), Reaganites raised the meaning of *accelerated* to an entirely
new level. The ill-fated Accelerated Cost Recovery System (ACRS)
allowed firms to write off most industrial equipment in just five
years—versus eight to 12 under previous law. Motor vehicles, re-
search-and-development equipment, and—would you believe?—
racehorses were further blessed with three-year depreciation lives.
And buildings, whose tax lives previously approximated their actual
lives (up to 40 years), could be written off in 15 years. Yes, 15 years.

In the wonderful world of tax shelters, as throughout the realm of
finance, faster is bigger. The reason is the time value of money. Since
sums received later are worth less than identical sums received sooner, it is better to get your cash flow early and your tax bill late. That
is precisely what accelerated depreciation accomplishes. By post-
poning the day of reckoning with the tax collector, faster write-offs
reduce the effective tax burden on capital, thereby rendering investments more attractive to prospective owners. That is the idea; and
the evidence is that it works in both theory and practice.

You can, however, have too much of a good thing. The depreciation allowed by ACRS came so quickly that it would have turned the
corporate tax into a corporate subsidy were allowances not scaled
back in 1982. For certain types of equipment, the subsidies could
only be called astounding. One study estimated that the 1981 law im-
plied effective subsidies of 233 percent on computers, 194 percent on
trucks, and 107 percent on aircraft. (The study did not compute the
subsidy on racehorses.) With a tax system like that, investors can do
well even without doing good.

Tax Break #2: Twenty years earlier, President Kennedy's economists invented the investment tax credit (ITC), a direct subsidy for the purchase of eligible equipment. The ITC has had an on-again, off-again history since 1962 and was "on" when President Reagan took office. It was made only slightly more generous in the orgy of tax cutting in 1981 and then was swept away by tax reform in 1986.

The ITC takes the K Mart approach to incentives: put industrial equipment on sale and businesses will buy more of it. Under a 10 percent investment tax credit, the purchase of a million-dollar generator generates an immediate $100,000 tax saving. So the machine costs the company just $900,000 net. Here again, evidence says that the approach works: the ITC does seem to stimulate investment. Such cannot confidently be said of the last two tax breaks I will mention.

Tax Break #3: Readers of this book will know that President Bush's favorite tax incentive is a preferentially low tax rate on capital gains. That this provision, which was stricken from the tax code in 1986, was in effect during the allegedly stagnant 1970s seems not to bother Bushmen. The argument is again straightforward—until you start to think about it, as we will shortly. *Some* of the returns on *some* investments (gee, the qualifiers are coming already) accrue in the form of capital gains. Taxing these gains more lightly will increase the allure of such investments, thereby encouraging an expansion of tax-favored activities.

Tax Break #4: I will mention just one last tax incentive for investors. (There are umpteen others.) A lower tax rate on corporate profits lets companies keep more of the earnings on their investments, whether those earnings come as ordinary income, capital gains, or whatever. Now there's an obvious incentive to invest, right?

Well, actually not. For one thing, a lower corporate tax rate reduces the value of depreciation allowances; so one tax break partially offsets the other. Further, firms generally borrow to finance their investments, and the interest they pay is tax-deductible. If the corporate tax rate falls, so do the tax deductions for interest; the after-tax cost of funds actually rises. For these reasons, economists place corporate tax rate cuts low on the hit parade of investment incentives—maybe right off the bottom.

For further information, please consult your tax adviser. For it is high time I started to reveal my reasons for skepticism. (What's that you say? They've not been hidden until now?)

AMPLE ROOM FOR DOUBT

To paraphrase Bette Davis in a different context: Fasten your seat belts. It's going to be a bumpy ride. My contention, in brief, is that America was sold a bill of goods in the 1980s, that the case for tax incentives has more holes than a Swiss cheese, and that we should

"It's 3 a.m.
Do you know where your package is? I do."

Dennis Connelly
Trace Agent, Boston

No matter what time of day or night you need to know about your packages,
documents, or freight—no matter where on earth they may be—our tracking networks
allow our Customer Service Agents to track them down for you. In seconds.

never have expected it to work. I proceed to a Baedeker of the holes.

The first problem is and was well understood by the capital-formation lobby. They even admitted it. If firms are energized to invest more, the resulting scramble for funds is likely to drive interest rates up. So some of the nascent enthusiasm for more investment will be snuffed out by higher interest rates. There are two possible responses, and oddly enough, one was given in the 1960s and the other in the 1980s.

The 1960s answer was easy money. By aggressively expanding the supplies of money and credit, the Federal Reserve System can nudge interest rates down. If, at the same time, tax incentives for investment are pushing interest rates up, the result may be a standoff. Very sensible. In fact, it is probably the right answer. Unfortunately, the Fed was never keen on the idea, and the grand scheme came apart when the Vietnam War made inflation the economic problem of the day and tight money the solution.

The 1980s answer was different. Easy money was out because everyone was frightened about inflation. Instead, powerful incentives to invest were to be the engine of growth, and powerful incentives to save were to be its fuel. The idea was that interest rates need not rise if saving and investment advance together. Again, very logical. The problem is that wishing doesn't make it so. The evidence suggests that Americans do not respond much, if at all, to incentives for saving. And this is one reason why the Reaganomic growth strategy was doomed to failure.

Personal saving as a share of after-tax income not only failed to rise in the 1980s, it actually fell. Now this does seem puzzling. Since lower tax rates really do increase the reward for saving, it seems to stand to reason that people will save more when tax rates are lower. Unfortunately, this is one place where Americans seem to defy common sense. One of the striking facts of U.S. economic history is that, as far as scholars can tell, the personal saving rate in this country has been more or less the same for more than a century. That covers a time-span in which the personal income tax rate in the top bracket ranged from zero (prior to 1913) to 92 percent (in 1952-1953) and then back down to 28 percent.

That fact alone should make you suspicious of claims that tax incentives will boost saving appreciably. But there is more. The surprising conclusion that households do not respond much to saving incentives did not surprise research economists in the early 1980s. The question had been studied extensively over the preceding decades, and with precious few exceptions, the answer was always the same: American savers barely respond. But evidence rarely persuades a true believer, and the Reagan team decided to bet that things would be different once morning dawned in America. Treasury secretary Donald Regan assured Congress that American families would save more than ever before. In fact, they saved less.

So the first criticism of the case for capital formation is that saving incentives are unlikely to work. Simple, but fairly devastating—as is the next one.

★★★

When I bought my home, I did not finance the entire purchase from savings. I borrowed money. When General Motors built the Saturn plant in Spring Hill, Tennessee, it too borrowed money. This is typical behavior. Individual investors have access to a national (shortly I will broaden this to an international) pool of capital from which to borrow. Who contributes to this pool? I have already mentioned household savers. Businesses save, too, whenever they retain earnings. And if you can imagine this, units of government contribute to the savings pool whenever their budgets are in surplus.

That brings me to the federal government's deficit—and to the second weakness in the case for capital formation. Every tax incentive the government provides costs the Treasury money and enlarges the budget deficit, at least in the short run. And larger budget deficits are withdrawals from the pool of national saving.

A few concrete numbers will illustrate. In round numbers, individuals saved about $180 billion in 1990 and corporations saved another $30 billion (net of depreciation allowances), for a total pool of net private saving of $210 billion. But the combined deficit of all levels of government was $125 billion, which drew $125 billion out of this pool, leaving just $85 billion to finance net private investment. If the government had devoted another $5 billion to saving incentives, and if those incentives had induced households to save $5 billion more—a generous estimate, given what we know—private saving would have risen to $185 billion but government dissaving would have grown to $130 billion. The same $85 billion would have been left for private investors to borrow.

In this hypothetical example, saving incentives work, but national saving fails to rise anyway because of the Treasury's revenue loss. In the real world, things are far worse: the Treasury still absorbs the revenue loss, but private saving hardly rises.

Investment incentives score better on this criterion. Many of them actually do stimulate investment. But once again, the government loses revenue. A tax incentive for investment that costs more than $30 billion per year—as the investment tax credit did when it was repealed in 1986—must stimulate at least that much in additional investment just to break even. If it does less, saving falls more than investment rises.

Revenue losses are greatly amplified if the saving or investment incentive creates tax loopholes, as they normally do. Ever wonder why America built so many office buildings and condominiums that stood vacant in the 1980s? Part of the answer is that the Accelerated Cost Recovery System allowed buildings to be depreciated in 15 years. Fifteen years? Even shoddy stuff lasts longer than that. As a direct result, buildings went up all over America not to shelter people but to shelter income. Syndicators found it embarrassingly easy (given the handsome fees they were charging) to design real estate partnerships that ran paper losses for top-bracket investors, who used those losses to put other income beyond the tax man's reach.

★★★

Everyone knows that the capital market is increasingly global. Treasurers of multinational corporations move millions around the globe with a few keystrokes. The U.S. government sells its bonds to Swiss bankers, Arab sheiks, and Japanese insurance companies. The money you deposit in Citibank or Bank of America may find its way to borrowers in Argentina, Singapore, or Turkey. All this is by now a familiar part of the financial furniture.

But it carries an ominous message for advocates of saving incentives. Even if Americans respond to tax incentives by saving more, and even if the additional saving exceeds the government's revenue loss—two dubious propositions, to be sure—there is no guarantee that investment will rise. Or, to put it more precisely, there is no guarantee that investment will rise within America's borders. In fact, we have every reason to believe that some portion will be put in place elsewhere. American saving incentives may spur investment in Japan or Mexico or the Philippines.

Now, there is nothing sinister about American funds financing investment abroad. Americans are hardly in a position to make a principled objection to cross-border flows of capital when we have grown so addicted to them ourselves. And American investors earn returns on their foreign investments. But U.S. taxpayers who foot the bill may wonder whether their pockets are being justifiably picked if the tax favors they provide for savers go partly to finance industrial expansion in Singapore.

★★★

Close your eyes and imagine an investment incentive that was truly neutral. It would subsidize all forms of capital formation equally. By enacting such a tax provision, Congress could boost investment without inducing firms to buy, say, more computers and fewer blast furnaces. Such decisions would be left where they belong: in corporate boardrooms, shops, and garages. For those who, like me, believe in competitive capitalism, it's a nice thought.

Now open your eyes to a starkly different reality. All real-world tax incentives distort the allocation of capital, sometimes grotesquely. The investment tax credit favors short-lived equipment. Capital gains preferences favor projects that generate capital gains. Jiggering depreciation schedules favors . . . well, whomever the tax-writing committees in Congress want to favor.

When tax considerations rather than economic merit start dictating investment patterns, a capitalist system is in deep trouble. Its invisible hand has been broken. Senator George Mitchell sensed this difficulty in the dark days of 1986 when tax reform appeared to be breathing its last in the Senate Finance Committee. After a day in which the committee decided to bless dental equipment, musical instruments, and caskets with more generous depreciation allowances than office furniture, communications satellites, and nuclear-power plants, he moaned, "Here are 20 politicians defining what assets are productive and what are not. At least in the Soviet Union they use economists for that." He might have added, "In America we are supposed to use capitalists."

All this adds up to a simple point: A bigger capital stock is not necessarily a better capital stock. If tax breaks raise the *quantity* of investment but decrease the *quality* of investment, we cannot be confident that industrial productivity will improve.

★★★

Nor is that the last problem. The next one is that most of the tax dollars the government gives away in saving or investment incentives are just that—giveaways, with no chance of increasing either saving or investment. Three examples will illustrate why.

1. *Rewarding Past Behavior.* By reducing the taxation of capital gains, we make old investments more profitable after the fact—a gift that will surely be appreciated by the recipients. But the dead hand of history is dead; we cannot go back and alter past behavior. From this day forward, we provide an added inducement to invest, as is wanted. But from this day backward, we merely shower gifts on past investments. Consequently, most of the lost tax dollars cannot possibly stimulate new investment. They serve only to enrich the owners of capital. One should perhaps not resist the conclusion that that is their purpose.

2. *Inviting Tax Arbitrage.* In the early 1980s, all wage earners were entitled to an Individual Retirement Account. Each year we were invited to reduce our taxable incomes by $2,000 simply by moving that amount to an account labeled IRA. *Good deal*, I thought. So, in all likelihood, did you. In fact, millions of Americans responded by shuffling funds to cut their tax bills by as much as $1,000 a year. And if you had the assets, you could take advantage of the gift without saving a dime.

Senator George Mitchell lost his fight against the 1986 tax reforms that favored special interests.

3. *Gifts for Doing Nothing.* Think about two very different companies, each investing $100 million per year. Moribund Manufacturing
Corporation, a mythical firm in the Rust Belt, is limping along; its investments are barely keeping its aging plant and equipment in good
repair while it seeks a buyer. Dynamic Growth Inc. is a high-tech
company investing full throttle and promising huge, though risky, returns to its owners. If the government offers a 5 percent investment
subsidy, each company will receive a check for $5 million. But will
they invest more? Moribund may not wish to throw more money
aboard the sinking ship; it might prefer to pay the $5 million out to
its beleaguered shareholders or use it to beef up its sickly balance
sheet. Dynamic, on the other hand, may be doing all the investing it
can handle and be unaffected—though delighted—by the $5 mil-
lion gift. The government gets thank-you notes, but not additional
investment.

The general point should be clear: every saving and investment
incentive rewards people for some things they would be doing anyway or have already done. There is no avoiding this, though some
tax breaks score better on this criterion than others. The consequence is that incentives for capital formation are expensive means to
their desired ends; in Washingtonspeak, they may offer little investment bang for the taxpayer's hard-earned buck.

★★★

All the preceding arguments pertain in one way or another to economic efficiency. But the previous chapter raised a quite different
problem, one that often dominates the political debate. Tax incentives
for saving and investment always redistribute income from the have-
nots to the haves. The reason is so elementary that it seems almost
condescending to state it. Nor would it ever have been questioned
save for the unending barrage of propaganda hurled by the vested interests. The whole idea behind saving and investment incentives is to
reduce the tax burden on capital. But, of course, the wealthy own
the capital; that's why we call them wealthy. So it is devilishly difficult to devise tax incentives for capital formation that do not redistribute income in favor of the rich. Not impossible, perhaps, but very
difficult. Plainly, the lawyers, accountants, and economists who design such incentives have not even tried.

THERE MUST BE A BETTER WAY

In sum, no one should be surprised that the growth strategy of the
1980s failed. There never was any reason to believe that tax incentives
would boost personal saving. Even if the medicine somehow worked,
it would probably not have raised national saving, for revenue losses
enlarge the government budget deficit. Even if national saving rose

on balance, some of the new investment would surely have been done outside the U.S. And on top of all that, tax breaks for savers are almost certainly regressive. We each keep score in our own way; but, to me, this adds up to a ringing condemnation of saving incentives.

Investment incentives hold more promise. There is at least reason to believe that offering an investment tax credit or accelerating depreciation will boost investment spending. However, those measures also cost the government revenue, including revenue that is squandered on giveaways to old investments, on investments that would be made anyway, and on egregious tax loopholes. They reduce economic efficiency by distorting free-market patterns of investment. And they widen income disparities by showering benefits on the people least in need. So the slim productivity gains from investment incentives come at high social cost. Is this the best we can do?

I hope not. But if we are to design and implement an alternative growth strategy with better prospects for success and fewer ill effects, we need some criteria. How else are we to tell a better policy from a worse one? Here we run smack up against a serious problem.

Children in our country, as in others, grow up with an intuitive understanding of what constitutes right and wrong in a moral sense. From their earliest years they are taught that it is wrong to lie, to steal, to harm another physically, or to covet their neighbors' possessions. (This last they ignore.) Though often honored only in the breach, these principles stand unquestioned, are enshrined in our laws, and provide a unit of account for moral bookkeeping.

Unfortunately, few children grow up recognizing good and bad economics. So the policies we get are an unprincipled and incoherent hodgepodge based on myths, homespun analogies, and unabashed self-dealing. Although legislators routinely pass laws that are premised on dreams or deception, amount to economic larceny, and do harm to society, few citizens call them to account. If we are to do better, the body politic needs a better sense of how to keep the economic score.

In a book published a few years ago, I suggested two simple guiding principles. The first is *the principle of efficiency*: that more is better than less, so that waste should be proscribed. The second is *the principle of equity*: that the poor are needier than the rich, and hence some social redistribution—toward the poor!—is appropriate. These two principles were joined metaphorically in the title of that book, *Hard Heads, Soft Hearts*, and I have been tacitly appealing to them both here. It is time to make that appeal explicit.

The hardheaded, softhearted approach leads to a concrete system of economic scorekeeping. Ask two questions. First, is the policy proposal likely to enhance or harm economic efficiency? If the latter, count a strike against it. Second, does the policy redistribute income in favor of the poor or the rich? If the latter, count another strike.

In this game, two strikes and you should be out. Policies that make the economy less productive while filling cups that are already brimming ought to be rejected in a democracy—and would be, I believe, if people grew up with a better-developed sense of economic right and wrong. Most of the tax incentives discussed in this chapter can be eliminated by precisely these criteria.

On the other hand, proposals that improve the prospects of society's underdogs while enhancing economic efficiency probably merit adoption. At least that should be the presumption.

It is over the difficult split decisions that political debate should take place. For example, suppose a cut in the top-bracket tax rate will make the economy more efficient, as is probably true. We are then confronted with a decision that is political in the best sense of the word. Is the efficiency gain worth the loss in social equity?

The same sort of question arises with measures that sacrifice efficiency to benefit the poor; Medicaid and housing subsidies are familiar examples. In such cases, we must ask whether the equity gains justify the efficiency losses. Over such questions reasonable men and women may disagree. The political arena is the proper place to work out such disagreements.

Reaganites were correct to emphasize efficiency and especially productivity in their growth strategy. But they were heartless to ignore the adverse distributional consequences of the policies they proposed. Is it fair to ask the poor to sacrifice for the rich? Similarly, 1960s-style romantic liberalism was right to value equality but was foolishly inattentive to economic efficiency. No nation, no matter how rich, can afford such profligacy.

What is needed in the 1990s is a growth strategy that is at once hardheaded and softhearted—a policy package that gets results, but not by taking them out of the hides of the poor and near-poor. The proper image of an economic policymaker is a person with the heart of a social worker but who looks at the world through green eyeshades, not rose-colored glasses. Impossible, you say? I think not.

AN AGENDA FOR GROWTH WITHOUT INEQUALITY

The first step down the road is to recall the kernel of truth in the conservative case for capital formation: more and better capital makes our labor force more productive. It's true. But precisely the same logic insists that more and better *labor* will make our *capital* resources more productive. It is hard to see how one could be true without the other.

So we have a choice. Shoring up capitalism need not start with capital, as the growth strategy of the 1980s blithely assumed. It can, instead, start with upgrading the quality of our labor force. Such a human-resource-based strategy has several distinct advantages. It aims its fire directly at improving the lot of those who have been left behind—the working people of America—rather than relying on trickle-down. It disavows tax loopholes that redistribute income in favor of the rich while distorting free-market decisions. And perhaps most important of all, there is real evidence that it might work.

Early in the previous chapter, I outlined four flawed premises on which the Reaganomic growth strategy rested. They were:

- Private capital formation is the key to growth.
- Government is an obstacle, not a partner.
- Tax cuts are the main route to better incentives.
- America needs unfettered cowboy capitalism.

The growth strategy that I propose for the 1990s could not be more different. It is, in fact, based on diametrically opposed premises. First, it places the development and utilization of human resources— human capital formation, if you will—at stage center in the growth process. Second, it sees government as a facilitator, not a hindrance. Third, while it seeks better incentives, it does not look for them in tax cuts but rather in changes in the way work is organized and workers are paid. Finally, it emphasizes what might be called *settler capitalism*—a philosophy that says we are here for the long haul and, in an important sense, are all in it together.

The choice, I must reiterate, is not between "doing something for capital" and "doing something for labor." Just as the growth strategy of the 1980s promised gains for labor, so does the suggested growth strategy for the 1990s promise gains for capital. The choice is rather between a capital-first strategy with trickle-down and a labor-first strategy with percolate-up. If my arguments are correct, the human-resource-based strategy will boost the productivity of capital. And that will pull investment along as surely as snow brings out children on sleds.

Every military planner knows that the grandest strategy is only as good as the tactics used to implement it. Lofty principles are useless without effective ways to put them into practice. It is to the tactics that I now turn.

"This is how big the world looks to our tracking network."

Judy Paynter
Corporate Programs Administrator, Colorado Springs

Whether you're shipping computer parts to Cologne or machine tools to Milan, our
state-of-the-art tracking network enables us to pinpoint the precise location of your shipment
almost anywhere on earth, within seconds. Proving that it's a small world, after all.

CHAPTER 4

THE CHILDREN ARE OUR FUTURE

When someone asked Earl Weaver, the longtime manager of the Baltimore Orioles, "What is the best play in baseball?," his answer was straightforward: a three-run home run. Lou Carnesecca, the highly successful basketball coach at St. John's University, says the secret to his success is simple: get good players.

Both these men are masters of their craft, so their answers may have been a trifle disingenuous. But each was making a simple and indisputably correct point. Good things are likely to happen to teams whose players can knock the ball over the wall or shoot the lights out of the basket.

So it is with a country's labor force. If a nation wants to squeeze the maximum productivity out of its human resources, it no doubt helps to provide employees with newer and better equipment. And just as Weaver's managing and Carnesecca's coaching surely contributed to their teams' successes, so creative business managers can coax more out of whatever labor resources they are given. (That is the subject of the next chapter.) However, good capital and good ideas work better when combined with a work force that is world class. If a nation is serious about raising its labor productivity, it should start with the raw materials.

This chapter asks what America can do to improve the quality of the labor pool from which our industry draws its employees. I begin at the bottom and work my way up. There are several good reasons for doing so.

First of all, elementary notions of social justice dictate that, at this juncture in U.S. history, efforts to build America's human-resource base start at the bottom. We saw in Chapter 2 that the lowest 20 percent of American households was left behind in the 1980s. Their already woeful standards of living slipped another notch—one they could ill afford. That the richest nation on earth has such a large, and by some accounts growing, underclass is a blot on the American dream.

America's underclass exists largely outside the mainstream of our society. When the children of the poor watch *The Cosby Show*, or even *Roseanne*, they are peering through an electronic window at a foreign land. In their neighborhoods, life is more like Hobbes's description in *Leviathan*: "poor, nasty, brutish, and short." Illiteracy, illegitimacy, drugs, and violence are the constants of everyday life there. When mothers in New York City's teeming housing projects send their children off to school, it is not with the middle-class salutation "Have a nice day," but with the hopeful admonition "Be safe." Upbringings like that leave scars on all but the strongest.

But the case for a bottom-up policy is based on more than social compassion. The human tragedy of America's underclass is also a shameful waste of precious economic resources. The U.S. puts itself at a crippling disadvantage by writing off the lowest 20 percent of its potential work force. Japan does not do that. Europe does not do that. Are Americans really arrogant enough to believe that 80 percent of us can win the competitive race while carrying the other 20 percent—even penuriously—on our backs?

As the 1990s progress, it will become increasingly expensive to consign the bottom 20 percent of the labor force to the social scrapheap. The reason is that America's youth population has declined remarkably in the last decade. We now have 15 percent fewer youths in the 16- to 24-year-old age bracket than we had just 10 years ago; and the youth population will remain this low for the balance of the century. Twenty years ago, demography posed a stern challenge to the U.S. economy: Could we successfully absorb the huge influx of young people who were about to enter the labor force? After some false starts, we met that challenge admirably. But now the forces of demography pose precisely the opposite problem. During the 1990s, America will have to fill millions of entry-level jobs—from hamburger-flippers to medical interns—from the thin ranks of the birth-dearth generation.

So the plight of the underclass offers a happy coincidence of interests between hardheaded calculation and softhearted compassion. If we continue to leave the children of the underclass on the bench, we are being not just meanspirited but also economically foolish. If we can somehow bring them into the mainstream, the whole team can be better off.

But how? What can we do? The war on poverty is already a quarter-century old, and its field marshals have precious few victories to their credit. Are there public-policy initiatives that really work? I think so. Indeed, of the many possible policy initiatives that can be dreamed up, there are a few for which persuasive evidence of effectiveness exists.

START YOUNG

Every now and then you come across an idea that is at once so simple and so powerful that it fundamentally and irretrievably changes your outlook on an issue. For me, that happened one day in 1987 while reading a newspaper account of a report on how to help the educationally disadvantaged. The report came from the Committee for Economic Development, a blue-ribbon business organization that represents what liberals like to call "enlightened conservative opinion." I immediately sent for a copy of *Children in Need*. That slender but fact-filled volume made an eloquent and persuasive case for a disarmingly simple principle: Start young. If you really want to have an impact on the cycle of poverty—not this year, not next, but in the more distant future, and in an enduring way—focus your energies on children, especially on very young children.

The wisdom behind this precept is so compelling that, as the poet William Blake said, it cannot be understood without being believed. Children are receptive, malleable, and resilient at life's start but grow progressively less so as they mature. Some experts in child development will tell you that it's all over by the age of 9 months. But you don't have to buy such an extreme position to see the basic point. A 16-year-old who has dropped out of school, given birth to or fathered a child, become dependent on drugs, and committed crimes may already be lost to society. At best, turning his or her life around will be a slow, expensive process with highly uncertain results. But a baby is a clean slate. A few gallons of milk, some elementary medical precautions, and a few hours of instruction on child-rearing cost a pittance but may yield an enormous social dividend.

It may seem cruel to suggest that we turn our backs on disadvantaged 16-year-olds, not to mention impoverished adults. And we should not. But a realist will recognize the limits of our ability to help these people; a holding action may be the best we can hope for. But there are no such limits with younger children.

Consider the story of Kim, a hypothetical but typical underclass child born with low birthweight to an illiterate, unwed, teenage mother. Kim's mother knows little or nothing about parenting. Indeed, she is still a child herself. The baby gets inadequate nourishment, rarely if ever sees a pediatrician, and receives little mental stimulation in its preschool years, and hence develops slowly. When school begins, Kim is ill-prepared to learn and quickly falls behind grade level.

Poor performance breeds low expectations and, in a well-known vicious circle, the child branded a slow learner soon ratifies the teachers' beliefs. After repeating the same grade several times, Kim drops out of school at age 15 or 16, barely literate. If she is a girl, she may become pregnant. If he is a boy, he may turn to crime. In either case, drug abuse is a common accompaniment.

Now the child is a problem—both for society and for him- or herself. Society's options at this point are severely limited. Prisons are boot camps where criminals hone their skills. Drug-rehabilitation programs show checkered results at best. And both are extremely expensive, which is a serious handicap in a nation that is less than generous toward its poor.

The government can accomplish much more if it intervenes earlier in life—with prenatal and postnatal nutrition and medical care, with counseling for young and expectant mothers, and with some kind of preschool education. More than common sense supports this argument; evidence abounds, as we shall see.

Nevertheless, social science is not natural science; we are not doing physics here. Putting a young child on track is a much more iffy proposition than putting a rocket into orbit. All of the programs whose virtues I am about to extol carry risks of failure. But there is no other way in social policy. We have no choice but to place a bet. A wise gambler will calculate the odds and bet shrewdly—with the evidence rather than against it.

Raising Better Babies

When I said start young, I meant young—even before birth. Too many unborn babies of the poor receive inadequate nutrition and prenatal care. The all-too-common result is low birthweight and the plethora of physical, mental, and psychological problems that go with it—including subsequent learning disorders. About 7 percent of all babies born in the United States, but about a quarter of all babies born to unwed mothers, now have low birthweight (less than five and a half pounds). We may not be able to do much about the chaotic environments into which some of these children are born, but low birthweight is the most curable of maladies. After all, milk is cheap.

The benefits and costs of prenatal programs speak for themselves. A recent congressional review of studies of the subject included numbers like the following:

• A study in Massachusetts estimated that each $1 spent on the prenatal component of the Women, Infants, and Children (WIC) program saved more than $3 in short-term hospital costs alone. Savings on long-term treatments were over and above this.

• Two studies of WIC in Missouri found that each $1 spent on prenatal care returned 49 to 83 cents in lower Medicaid expenses within the first weeks of life. An earlier study estimated that the savings during the infant's first year were about $2.

• The Institute of Medicine estimated that each $1 spent on prenatal services for low-income pregnant women saved $3.38 in costs of care for low-birthweight infants.

• At the University of California at San Diego in 1985, hospital care for babies born with no prenatal care cost an average of $2,200 more than corresponding care for babies whose mothers received adequate prenatal care. But such care cost only about $1,000 per pregnancy.

• A 1984 study of some 120,000 births in Kansas found that only 5 percent of women with adequate prenatal care gave birth to low-birthweight babies versus 12 percent of women with inadequate care. Medical costs for infants requiring intensive care averaged $15,000.

• The Colorado Health Department found that only 5 percent of women who received early and continuous prenatal care had premature babies, as compared to 28 percent of women who received no care. It estimated that each $1 spent on prenatal care could save $9 on medical expenses due to prematurity.

And so it goes. Even allowing for generous margins of error, these are stunningly high returns—the kinds that make venture capitalists drool. And none of these calculations place any monetary value on the reductions in pain and suffering, not to mention infant mortality, that prenatal care can yield. Failure to exploit such bountiful opportunities is a shameful waste, for the programs eventually save the government more than they cost. Yet about 10 percent of black babies are born to mothers who receive late or no prenatal care. And the WIC program reaches only about half the eligible population.

It needn't be so. New Jersey's WIC program increased enrollment by 24 percent in a single year through aggressive marketing techniques. And WIC's nationwide budget has been raised several times in recent years despite overall budget stringency. In this case, we seem to be moving in the right direction. We just need to move faster.

An equally strong case can be made for spending more on infant and toddler care. Doing so is not only cost-effective, but some of the necessary steps are embarrassingly elementary. For example, a 1984 study at the University of North Carolina estimated that each $1 spent on the Childhood Immunization Program saves $10 in subsequent medical costs. A year later, a more specific study of the measles, mumps, and rubella vaccine found a benefit-cost ratio of 14 to 1. This is probably one of America's great success stories, since most of our children are immunized against the major childhood diseases. But a significant minority misses out. As I write this, a measles epidemic is spreading in Pennsylvania and New Jersey. Something is amiss when the percentage of American households with TV sets exceeds the percentage of children that have been vaccinated against polio.

But we can do more than give injections. After birth, many babies of the poor continue to be undernourished and receive little or no medical attention. Many of their mothers know little about child-rearing. The result is that too many disadvantaged children develop poorly—physically, mentally, and emotionally—and are destined to be failures in school.

Getting food and medical care to more children at risk through programs like WIC is one obvious step. But taking it may, as I indicated before, require aggressive marketing efforts, for many of the mothers are apparently too ill informed, neglectful, or distrustful of government to step forward and claim benefits to which they are entitled.

Beyond this, there are some more subtle steps that can be taken early in life, steps that would help lay the groundwork for success in school. The results of a small-scale experiment in Harlem in the 1960s were particularly striking. Over the course of several months, about 250 2- and 3-year-olds were exposed to a few hours of creative play with trained professionals. Another set of statistical controls received no such exposure. Several years later, just before the children entered school, the experimental subjects were still significantly ahead of the controls in several measures of performance and mental development. A lot for a little, it seems to me.

A HEAD START ON EDUCATION

Moving up to 3- and 4-year-olds, we find what may be one of our nation's greatest missed opportunities: preschool education. Less than 0.5 percent of our national spending on education now goes to children under the age of 6. That would be a sensible allocation of funds if preschool were only a glorified form of babysitting. But the evidence points to the opposite conclusion: that investments in preschooling for 3- or 4-year-olds pay handsome dividends.

Project Head Start may be the greatest success story of the Great Society. It includes not only preschooling but also health, nutritional, and social services for needy children. And it has been studied extensively over the 26 years of its existence. The studies do not always agree, but a fair summary of the evidence might go as follows. Participation in Head Start increases IQ scores and perhaps the cognitive abilities of disadvantaged 3- and 4-year-olds. However, these gains tend to last only until the second or third grade and then disappear as other kids catch up. Nonetheless, Head Start children seem to perform better throughout their school careers: they attend more regularly, drop out less, earn higher grades, and so on.

Most astonishingly (and most controversially, given the paucity of data), children who have been put through Head Start or similar programs seem to enjoy more socioeconomic success in their teenage years and later—some 10 to 20 years after the program. They are more likely to graduate from high school and attend college, less likely to commit crimes, become pregnant, or go on welfare. They also appear to earn higher wages and experience less unemployment. These long-delayed benefits are, of course, devilishly difficult to measure, because following the lives of disadvantaged youths over a decade or two is a daunting task and therefore rarely done. Hence our knowledge of these matters rests on a slender database.

For example, a follow-up study 16 years later of 178 children in Harlem Head Start (by then, aged 19 to 21) found that participants were twice as likely as a control group to be employed, 50 percent more likely to have graduated from high school, and 33 percent more likely to have gone on to further education. These are truly impressive gains registered after a lapse of 16 years.

The most carefully designed, closely monitored, and thoroughly evaluated preschool program of all, however, was not a Head Start program. That honor goes to the Perry Preschool Program in Ypsilanti, Michigan. The subjects in this scientifically designed experiment, which was conducted between 1962 and 1967, were 3- and 4-year-olds selected from a poor, black neighborhood near the Perry Elementary School on the south side of Ypsilanti, a suburb of Detroit. Far from selecting the most promising preschoolers, program directors made sure their subjects were particularly disadvantaged by rejecting children whose parents were too well educated or held jobs that were too good, or if they were too well housed. The kids who remained eligible were given an IQ test, and only those with IQs between 60 and 90 were selected for the program. Statistically speaking, these children were destined for failure.

The 123 boys and girls so selected were randomly divided into two groups. Fifty-eight were given either one or two years of high-quality preschool education—about two and a half hours per day over a period of seven and a half months per year. Parents were also involved at home. The other 65 were used as statistical controls and received no special education. Amazingly, researchers managed to follow all but two of the students—including all 58 who received the preschooling—until at least age 19. Costs and benefits were totted up and evaluated in inflation-corrected dollars using a 3 percent real interest rate. That is precisely the kind of calculation economists want done as part of a proper cost-benefit analysis.

The findings were eye-opening. Because the program used such a low student-teacher ratio—one staff member for every five or six children—the costs ran high: about $4,800 per student per year when expressed in 1981 dollars (which the study used as its basis for comparison). That is more than Head Start costs, even today. But the benefits were vastly higher. For one year in the program, the estimated measured benefits through age 19 were more than $7,300—mostly in the form of lower educational costs (the children needed fewer special services) and less crime (counting only the economic losses, not the fear, trauma, etc., imposed on victims).

After age 19, the gains mostly took the form of higher projected earnings and taxes paid, with some further contribution from lower crime rates. Some earnings advantage for the preschool group over the control group was already apparent by age 19, even though more of the former were still in school. But most of the estimated earnings gap had to be extrapolated based on patterns of earnings by educational attainment for blacks. Such a calculation is surely subject to a considerable margin of error. For what it is worth, the authors of the study projected subsequent earnings gains of $23,800 over the lifetime of a typical child in the program and about another $3,300 savings in lower welfare and crime costs.

The total social return from an initial investment of $4,800 thus topped $34,000. Quite an investment! Even from the crass standpoint of the government budget, forgetting about any benefits to the children, the program was a clear winner. It led to higher tax receipts and lower schooling, and welfare costs that far exceeded the initial outlays on preschooling.

Further benefits, ones that cannot readily be expressed in dollars and cents, also flowed from the program. Children who received preschooling earned significantly higher grades in school (more than one-third of a letter grade), were more likely to graduate from high school (67 percent versus 49 percent) and go to college or vocational school (38 percent versus 21 percent), and the girls were only about half as likely to become pregnant by age 19. About 45 percent of the children who went through the program were self-supporting by age 19 (versus 25 percent in the control group), and only 19 percent had been on welfare (versus 41 percent of the controls).

All these are remarkable legacies from a little education received at ages 3 and 4. Our enthusiasm for the results must, of course, be tempered by the small and special nature of the experiment. It was run by a highly professional and dedicated staff and involved only 123 kids. All the children were black, came from the same town, were economically disadvantaged, and had low IQs. Special, indeed. But would anyone argue that the Perry children were easy marks for a preschool program? These kids started life with a losing hand and, once they left the program, attended the same schools, lived in the same neighborhoods, and were subject to the same influences as their peers. If preschooling had such remarkably durable effects on the Perry children, it is not unreasonable to think it might work as well or better elsewhere.

The Perry program was not, of course, the last word on cost-effectiveness. Obviously, its target population was very special, so we cannot simply generalize its findings. It also used a low student-teacher ratio; programs with a higher ratio might well be more economical. Finally, the evaluators of the Perry program found that the benefits of the second year of preschooling were negligible, although the costs were roughly the same as for the first year, suggesting that the second year is largely wasteful. But some other research suggests that when it comes to preschool years, the more the merrier. We do not have definitive answers to these and other questions of program design. But we do know enough to make it a good bet that investments in preschooling for more children at risk will pay off handsomely.

At present, Head Start enrolls only about one-third of the 3- to 5-year-old children living in poverty—up from less than 20 percent just a few years ago. That percentage should rise further in the next few years since Congress, in a rare fit of wisdom, has authorized full funding of Head Start by 1994. However, the parlous state of the federal budget makes it unlikely that the authorized sums will actually be appropriated. They were not in 1991, for example. Skimping on Head Start does not serve the interests of taxpayers. It is certainly pound-foolish and may not even be penny-wise.

Head Start is not an expensive program; its budget for fiscal year 1991 is less than $2 billion. Based on actual per-pupil costs, and assuming that children split fifty-fifty between Head Start's full-day and half-day programs, it would take about $3.8 billion to offer Head Start services to every at-risk 4-year-old in America and $7.5 billion to include 3-year-olds as well. Because 100 percent coverage is well beyond our reach, we are probably talking about an increase of the Head Start budget of $1 billion to $3 billion per year, or $4 to $12 annually from each citizen. This is certainly something America can afford. Indeed, it is a bargain we cannot afford to pass up.

I have posed the case for early intervention strictly in economic terms. Even looked at through the needed green eyeshades, the case looks pretty strong. In my experience, however, unvarnished economic logic rarely prevails in the political arena. As Gypsy Rose Lee knew, you gotta have a gimmick in politics—or a slew of well-heeled lobbyists. Early intervention for children at risk has neither.

Fortunately, the cold economic arguments are buttressed by a moral case that is white-hot and by a political appeal that is all but irresistible. After all, what group in our society tugs more strongly on our hearts than children? Early intervention is, quite literally, a motherhood issue. It is hard to believe that America cannot muster the political will to do more for its childen in need.

Promoting Literacy and Numeracy

Education is on everyone's list of growth-enhancing policies—and should be. Even a cursory look around the world reveals an undeniable association between education and income levels. Better-educated nations are richer. But what does this correlation prove? The seemingly obvious conclusion is that more education leads to higher productivity. But we must remember that just as chickens produce eggs, so do eggs produce chickens. The question is, which is cause and which effect? With education and income, as with chickens and eggs, we must look in both directions.

Certainly, part of the strong correlation between a nation's average income and its average educational attainment simply reflects the fact that education is a luxury that wealthier countries can better afford. But that cannot be the whole story. Volumes of research attest that education—at least some forms of education—boosts productivity directly, especially in countries where average educational attainment is low.

Nonetheless, this book devotes relatively little space to education—for three reasons. First, my intent is to call attention to growth policies you might not otherwise think about. But all of us have been thoroughly schooled on the virtues of schooling. Second, how best to reform the educational system is a contentious issue that demands a book-length treatment—a book that should be written by someone more expert in this area than I. For example, controversial new research suggests that smaller class sizes may be cost-effective—a reversal of what had become the conventional wisdom in educational circles. Third, and finally, the United States already has a high average level of educational attainment, at least if you measure time spent in school and are not too fussy about quality. So it is more than a little disingenuous for me, as a professor, to claim that sprinkling more education dollars across the board is the route to economic salvation. We must be more selective.

Where, then, can we get the largest productivity bang for our educational bucks? My hunch—it is not much more than that—is that two areas hold out the most promise: improving basic literacy and providing more scientific and technical training.

Estimates of the number of illiterates in the contemporary United States vary widely and are hotly contested. Partisans in the debate exaggerate or belittle the problem, depending on what policy measure they are promoting or opposing. But no matter how it is measured, illiteracy in the U.S. today is shamefully high for a nation as wealthy as ours. Perhaps 20 million to 40 million Americans over the age of 18 are either functionally illiterate or just barely literate. By comparison, illiteracy is almost unknown in Japan—and their language has thousands of characters and is written both horizontally and vertically!

How can the United States field a capable blue-collar labor force when a substantial minority of its workers cannot read or write or do arithmetic? Would Earl Weaver have won with singles hitters or Lou Carnesecca prevailed with players his own size? When you talk to top executives of major American manufacturing companies, one of their first pleas is the same as Carnesecca's: Get me better players. They bemoan the scarcity of literate blue-collar workers. Economist Lester Thurow points out that German and Japanese factories use "unlocked" machine tools that can be adjusted by workers when there is a simple malfunction, whereas U.S. manufacturers use less flexible "locked" machine tools because our blue-collar workers cannot be taught the simple programming skills needed to unlock them. When equipment breaks, work ceases until the mechanic comes.

To reduce illiteracy, we will almost certainly have to spend more on compensatory and remedial education. We will probably have to raise teacher salaries and do other things (such as ensuring school safety) to make both teaching and learning in inner-city schools more attractive, or at least possible. In addition, we would probably be better off if small schools with small classes replaced inner-city behemoths with crowded classrooms. All this will cost piles of money.

Whereas a campaign against illiteracy would offer the most help to those at the bottom of the economic pyramid, greater efforts in science and math would do the most good at the top.

The economist Lester Thurow has called the U.S. educational system a disaster. His ideas for reform include competitive wages for teachers.

No single fact can convey the nature of a complex problem, but the following comparison between the U.S. and Japan comes close. In the U.S., the number of lawyers and accountants coming out of our schools each year roughly equals the number of engineers. By contrast, Japan produces roughly 100 engineers for every lawyer or accountant. Should we be surprised, then, that Japan leads the world in engineering while the U.S. leads the world in litigation? Legend has it that when the U.S. government announced tougher standards for automobile emissions in the 1970s, Japanese executives summoned their engineers while American executives summoned their lawyers. If the legend is true, our side has something to worry about.

America's problems with science start early in the schools and continue right up to the top. International comparisons of mathematical and scientific achievement consistently place American schoolchildren well down the list while Japanese children always score near the top. The most recent rankings of science achievement, for example, put American 14-year-olds 13th out of 17 nations (tied with Thailand). At the college level Americans do much better, and at the graduate-school level we surely offer the very best education there is. Nothing abroad comes close to MIT, Cal Tech, Harvard, or Princeton. The problem here is that too few American youths opt for scientific careers. Our fine graduate programs in science and engineering are filled with foreign students while American kids flock to law and business schools.

What to do? We knew what to do in 1957, when Sputnik shocked us out of our lethargy. The productivity growth gap is in some ways more insidious than the missile gap we supposedly faced in 1957. If we don't improve our growth performance, we are sure to lose. A Sputnik-like response is called for—and I mean a national campaign for more and better science education from top to bottom.

At the bottom, the main need is for better—better teachers, better instructional materials, and better scientific education from kindergarten through high school. Despite the natural curiosity of youth, our school system manages to chase kids out of science en masse—and quickly. Nor do they learn much while they remain. We need to do a better job of instilling an interest in science in children—or, rather, of not killing it. That will mean, among other things, pay scales for science and math teachers that are competitive enough to attract more talent into teaching. It may also mean more extensive cooperation with businesses and universities, which have the scientific talent to lend to the public schools. In general, it will mean more creativity and less educational bureaucracy.

At the top, the main need is for more—mainly more undergraduate and graduate students choosing scientific educations. Students, like everyone else, respond to incentives. In the post-Sputnik era, generous graduate fellowships under the National Defense Education Act helped attract thousands of our best and brightest into scientific careers. Perhaps the time is ripe to repeat the experiment. With the financial industry in disarray, the legal industry laboring under well-publicized oversupply, and both professions in vague disrepute, it may be easier to attract America's youth into science and engineering now than it was in the 1980s. It would certainly do our economy no harm if the next generation turned to creation rather than manipulation.

So those are the two educational initiatives that seem most promising to me: a drive for greater literacy at the bottom and a collateral drive for more scientific education at the top. Neither is fusion in a jar. Their benefits are hard to measure. And their financial returns almost certainly fail to equal those on the early-intervention programs discussed earlier in this chapter. But does anyone seriously doubt that America would have a more capable work force in the year 2010 if we started doing these things now?

"We serve more gourmet meals than most restaurants."

James Mercurio
Account Executive, Dallas

Thanks to an innovative service called Dinners a la Federal Express,[sm]
fine food merchants eager to expand their markets can ship anything from
live lobsters to pecan pies, fresh to practically anywhere in the country.
It's enough to satisfy even the heartiest new business appetites.

CHAPTER
5

USING OUR HUMAN RESOURCES

In a memorable vignette from *Sesame Street*, two Muppets struggle to reach some fruit hanging from a high limb. One is too short. The other, though tall enough, has rigid arms that prevent him from eating the fruit. After some awkward moments, one of them gets a brilliant idea: Let's work together. The tall Muppet reaches the fruit, and the one with the flexible arms feeds it to both of them. Basking in the glow of the moment, the two Muppets ponder a name for their momentous discovery. "Let's call it *Shirley*," suggests the first. "No," says the other, "let's call it *cooperation*."

The premise of this chapter is that American management and labor have ignored the lesson of the Muppets. Even with the capital and labor resources now on hand, many American businesses might be able to boost productivity dramatically by reorganizing their workplaces to create more Shirley—er, cooperation—between labor and management. Furthermore, such a transformation need not raise costs. Indeed, in many instances it might lower them. Labor-management cooperation may provide the legendary free lunch.

Japan provides a fascinating case in point. For many years Americans looked east at the economic miracle unfolding there and attributed it to massive investments in capital. The Japanese were, after all, ahead of us in robotics, while much of our plant and equipment was antiquated. No wonder their productivity was growing so much faster than our own, we reasoned. By now, however, Japan's industrial equipment is not much younger than ours, and robotics have failed to revolutionize American industry.

In the decade since the publication of the Japan expert William Ouchi's *Theory Z*, more and more Americans have come to realize that the secret to Japanese industrial success lies not in the way they manage capital, but in the way they manage people. This message, now widely accepted among thoughtful Japanese, is gradually seeping into the American business conscience. The challenge is to turn the seepage into a flood—and fast. A simple story illustrates how much may be at stake.

Nippon Electric Company (NEC) was experiencing an unusually large number of defects in one of its semiconductor plants. No one could figure out why. The machinery appeared to be in excellent shape. The work force received the same training, and the quality-control program was the same as in the company's other plants. Yet an inordinate number of rejects were coming off the line.

One day, as the company's engineers were pondering the problem, a young woman walking to work had to stop at a railroad crossing near the factory as a long freight train rumbled by. Like everyone who worked at the plant, she knew about the quality-control problem. Because she had been trained extensively and had rotated through most positions on the factory floor, she was familiar enough with the technology of chip-making to get an idea: Perhaps vibrations from the train were causing the problem.

That day, she shared the thought with her foreman, who agreed it had merit. So did the plant manager, who decided to have a trench dug around the factory and filled with water to cushion the vibrations when the trains passed. It worked. The rate of defects declined drastically. Only then was Tokyo headquarters informed of the solution.

After telling this story, a famous American industrialist mused over what might have happened if the factory had been owned by a large, bureaucratic U.S. corporation. First, the worker might never have been told of the dimensions of the defect problem. Second, even if she was, she probably would not have known enough about chip-manufacturing to realize that vibrations could imperil the process. Third, even if she did, she might have thought, *That's management's problem, not mine.* Even if she didn't, she might have encountered resistance within the factory. With apathetic fellow workers, an indifferent foreman, and no quality circle or access to management, the alert worker might have found it difficult to get her message heard.

Suppose, however, that she somehow overcame these obstacles and convinced management that she was right. At this point, the problem would have been referred to corporate headquarters. There, after many meetings, a committee would have been set up to study the question. After long delays and huge expenditures, a typically American decision would have been reached: the giant company should purchase the railroad and shut it down!

If you think the first scenario leads to a more productive society than the second, please read this chapter.

Cooperation is a warm and fuzzy word. Only boors and egomaniacs oppose it overtly. The real question is not whether labor and management should cooperate, but rather what concrete steps workers and executives can take to turn factories, offices, and shops into more cooperative work environments. In this chapter, I suggest two: profit-sharing and employee involvement. In a literal sense, the two ideas are separable; either can be utilized without the other. But so can butter and toast. The truth is that they form a mutually supporting pair. Each works better in the presence of the other.

SHARE AND SHARE ALIKE

In the early 1980s, a series of technical papers by a brilliant economic theorist named Martin Weitzman sketched an exciting new idea. Weitzman theorized that if workers received part of their compensation in profit-sharing rather than in straight wages, firms would be less inclined to lay them off when business conditions worsened. Why? Because slumps reduce profits and therefore would automatically scale back profit-sharing payments to employees, thereby paring labor costs without the need for layoffs. Widespread profit-sharing, Weitzman reasoned, might reduce unemployment, thus ridding capitalism of one of its least attractive features.

Persuasive, I thought. So, after the publication of Weitzman's book *The Share Economy* in 1984, I set out to use the power of the press to publicize his idea. Op-ed pieces in *The Boston Globe* and *The Washington Post* in 1985 were noticed in several quarters—including *The New York Times*, which editorialized that Weitzman's theory was "the best idea since Keynes." The intellectual boom in profit-sharing was on. Soon British ministers and Democratic presidential hopefuls (the Democrats seem to produce only hopefuls) were touting profit-sharing as a tonic for their respective ailing economies.

While all this was going on, an idea was germinating in my head. Wouldn't giving workers a share of the company's profits help align the interests of labor and management, as the original advocates of profit-sharing had thought decades ago? Wouldn't that automatically reduce conflict and create a more cooperative workplace? Might not such fine atmospherics boost worker morale and—most important—productivity? Weitzman's theory gave no answer. But the basic idea seemed simple and compelling. After all, in a capitalist society the profit motive is the wellspring of productivity and innovation. But large companies forget this simple lesson and pay their workers for hours spent on the job, not for output produced or profits generated. Can that be the best way to motivate the work force? Wouldn't employees have stronger incentives to perform if part of their pay were linked to company profits? Sounds plausible. But is it true?

A lucky coincidence gave me a chance to find out. One day in 1988 the phone rang. As part of a larger project, the Brookings

Institution wished to sponsor a volume of research on whether alternative labor-compensation systems affect productivity. Would I manage the endeavor for them—define the questions, select a team of researchers, and see that the work was done? Normally I would turn such an offer down flat; in the research business, I am labor, not management. But here was an opportunity to get others to answer a question that had bothered me for years. I took the job.

The result was a conference in March 1989 followed in 1990 by a book, *Paying for Productivity: A Look at the Evidence*. The research summarized there made a believer of me and, I think, of others as well. (It also opened my eyes to the importance of worker participation. But that's getting ahead of my story.) While not all indications were favorable, the preponderance of evidence from case studies, opinion surveys, simple statistical comparisons, and complex econometric investigations all pointed in the same direction: Profit-sharing appears to boost productivity. Increases of 3 to 11 percent seem most typical, though there are exceptions in both directions.

Boosting productivity by 3 to 11 percent would not constitute a third Industrial Revolution. But if such gains were not entirely consumed by labor—a big if, to be sure—they would transform a company's bottom line beyond recognition. And they come cheaply. No expensive investment in plant and equipment is necessary; no painstaking improvements in work-force quality are required. All that is needed is a change in the way the company compensates its employees—a veritable flick of the pen. This comes deliciously close to getting something for nothing.

If the research is correct, the implications for American industry are far-reaching. But is it correct? And why does profit-sharing sometimes fail? Mindful of my earlier admonition that softhearted people take care to be hardheaded, we should watch for flaws in the argument, for each potential flaw warns us of something that must be done to make profit-sharing work. Critics have raised three principal objections.

First comes the free-rider problem. It is no mystery why single-employee companies use profits as a motivator while large companies typically do not. To an owner-manager, the link between effort and income is clear and unmistakable; and the lure of riches has a wonderful way of concentrating the mind. But to an employee of a company with, say, 10,000 workers, the corresponding connection is dim at best. Suppose Joe Sixpack's hard work boosts his company's profits by $10,000. If employees are entitled to a 20 percent share of the profits, Joe's pro rata share will be 20 cents. Some incentive! So if Joe prefers the easy life, he is likely to free-ride on the efforts of others. After all, he gets a tiny share of any profits they generate. But, of course, if all employees leave the hard work to the proverbial other guy, the enterprise is in deep trouble. No one can free-ride on a train that does not move.

Nothing can eliminate the free-rider problem entirely, for it inheres in bigness. But companies can practice damage control by instilling a spirit of community, a sense of belonging to something bigger—perhaps even of pride in the company. As Weitzman and his coauthor, Douglas Kruse, wrote, "[It is] not enough for management just to install a profit-sharing system and walk out the door. To get the productivity-enhancing effects, something more may be needed—something akin to developing a corporate culture that emphasizes company spirit [and] promotes group cooperation. . . . " Accomplishing this may take a great deal of effort by both labor and management. So profit-sharing is not really a free lunch. One main route to team spirit, of course, is to create a more participatory work environment—a point to which I will return shortly.

The second problem with profit-sharing is that workers may be loath to put part of their wages at risk, especially if they distrust management. One reason workers are workers and capitalists are capitalists is that the former are less willing to bear risks than the latter. Yet profit-sharing shifts some of the risks of business from capital back to labor.

The severity of this problem no doubt varies from firm to firm and from time to time. So profit-sharing is not for all times and places. But workers worried about the risks of profit-sharing should understand that their jobs are not now riskless assets. Under the conventional wage system, their main peril is the risk of layoff. Under profit-sharing, layoffs would be comparatively rare, but wage-rate risk would be greater. Is that so bad a trade?

Furthermore, well-designed profit-sharing plans can limit a worker's financial risk. Most profit-sharing plans in the U.S. grant employees shares in the company and often immobilize them in the pension fund until retirement. This is a mistake, for it burdens workers with a terribly undiversified portfolio. If the company runs into trouble some years down the road, workers may lose not only their jobs but also a sizable chunk of their life savings. Many workers have suffered precisely this fate. Periodic cash payments tied to profits would put workers in a much less vulnerable position because they would not be compelled to hold their savings in company stock.

The third problem is that workers who are asked to bet part of their income on the company's profits may feel entitled to a voice in how the company is run. Indeed, they probably are entitled, just as stockholders are entitled to a vote. A comprehensive program of worker participation is one way to give employees such a voice. But critics of profit-sharing fret that any infringement on management's authority will impair the efficiency of capitalist enterprise.

Is this true? Does worker participation normally undermine productivity? I think not. Indeed, a strong case can be made for precisely the opposite proposition: that employee involvement enhances productivity. Here goes.

GETTING INVOLVED

A production worker in an auto-parts plant told *Business Week*, "Everybody that works here is competitive. We're willing to work long hours. We want to be multiskilled and learn how we can make the product better so we can be the best in quality and service to the customer. And if we do that, this plant will be around a long time."

Who employs him? Toyota? No. Honda? No. But those are good guesses. In fact, the gung-ho employee is Robert Hubble, who works at Corning Inc.'s automotive-filter plant in Blacksburg, Virginia.

Corning has perhaps taken employee involvement as far as any American company. Pressure from foreign competition in the mid-1980s forced top executives to contemplate radical changes. According to executive vice-president Norman Garrity, management concluded that "if you don't pay attention to the people aspects, such as empowering workers to make decisions, you could only get 50 percent of the potential benefit of restructuring." So Corning started to pay attention.

When the Blacksburg plant opened in 1989, it had the latest equipment, to be sure. But that was not all. Plant manager Robert Hoover had reduced the number of job classifications from the traditional 47 to only four, so the carefully selected production workers could rotate jobs and acquire new skills. (In Marysville, Ohio, Honda has gone even further: there is just one blue-collar job category.) Work was organized into self-directing teams, which enabled Corning to eliminate several layers of management. The Blacksburg plant is run by just three managers.

The results exceeded the company's expectations. Despite the exceptionally high costs of training its all-new work force, the plant turned a profit in its first year of operation. At Blacksburg, a production line can be retooled to produce a different kind of filter in one-sixth of the time it takes a traditional plant. And the employees, despite putting in rigorous 12½-hour workdays (either three or four per week), are delighted. "We have a lot of responsibility," says Hubble, "but that makes me feel good."

Corning is also feeling good and is currently converting its other 27 factories to team-based production. Earnings have soared, and CEO James Houghton says, "In my gut I can tell you a large part of our profit increase has come about because of our embarking on this way of life." Hoover believes the secret was simple: "Challenging people instead of forcing them to do dumb, stupid jobs."

Precisely. The traditional view of labor's role in a modern economy comes down to us from Frederick Taylor and Henry Ford. Extreme specialization is seen as the route to high productivity. The worker is but a cog in a wheel, a replaceable part. Good employees need brawn, not brains; obedience, not initiative. They must be given very precise instructions and then perform their small tasks by rote.

The alternative view comes from Japan and is gradually making inroads in American industry. The worker is seen as a thinking being who can and should contribute ideas, not just muscle, to the production process. To take advantage of the intimate knowledge each employee has of his job, even blue-collar workers should be allowed some discretion and control over how their work is organized. In the Japanese view, an experienced worker "gives wisdom to the machine" by constantly improving his equipment and its use. That process, according to some Japanese economists, is the heartbeat of Japan's extraordinary industrial dynamism.

Now ask yourself two questions. First, under which system would you rather work? Second, which system do you think generates higher productivity and greater product quality? Corning thinks it knows.

When Americans think about employee involvement—which is not often enough—they usually think of prominent manufacturers like Corning. But the concept can work in surprising places.

Henry Ford's assembly-line method of mass production enabled him to price the Model T at only $500 in 1913.

Hampton Inn is a rapidly growing chain of economy hotels whose competitive edge stems from the money-back guarantee it offers to any dissatisfied customer. According to CEO Ray Schultz, "The secret to making the guarantee work is giving our employees the authority to implement it. The Hampton Inn program authorizes all employees—not just the hotel manager or the front-desk personnel—to take whatever action is necessary to keep the customer satisfied." If a housekeeper finds a guest unable to get into her room because the key will not work, she is authorized to get a new key, change the lock, or assign the guest to a new room. If everything else fails, she is even empowered to offer a night's refund on the spot. Guests react well to the system and, just as important, so do employees.

These and other success stories show that a minority of American businesses are already making excellent use of worker participation to raise productivity, cut costs, improve quality, and boost sales. Unfortunately, systematic statistical evidence is hard to come by because participation comes in a bewildering variety of shapes and sizes. It can mean anything from purely consultative mechanisms like quality circles, to representation on workers' councils or corporate boards, to substantive involvement in decision-making on the shop floor. No two participatory programs are exactly alike, and so no two should be expected to have the same effect on productivity.

However, the evidence to date clearly looks favorable. A 1990 survey of research on the subject turned up 29 studies varying widely in both method and quality. Of these, 14 detected either large or lasting productivity improvements from worker participation, only two found negative effects, and 13 yielded more ambiguous results: Productivity gains were either small or short-lived. Evidence like that will not convince a confirmed disbeliever. But, like executives at Corning and Hampton Inn, I am not inclined to disbelieve. At the very least, the evidence certainly makes it easier to believe that participation helps rather than hurts productivity.

International evidence points in the same direction. The most prominent example is Japan, where extensive employee involvement in shop-floor decision-making is the norm, not the exception. And it seems to work wonderfully well. Indeed, several observers of the Japanese economy believe it to be the principal source of their ferocious competitiveness. Of course, Japanese and American businesses do many things differently, so the comparison is not clean. Nonetheless, the fact that Japanese management has made (almost) the same system work in their U.S. factories—with American workers— should make us stand up and take notice.

A Tale of Two Countries

Consider the contrasting experiences of two production workers, whom we'll call Ken and Kenichi. Each is hired directly out of high school by a large manufacturing firm. There the similarity ends.

Ken goes to work for Greenville Gadget Corporation, which has a seniority-based layoff policy that it invokes freely whenever sales slump. Layoffs are a routine part of life, as are dismissals of employees who perform poorly. So Ken views his job as a port of entry into the fluid American labor market. He does not expect to remain at Greenville more than a year or two.

The company feels the same way about Ken. It gives him minimal and very specialized on-the-job training: Two days of orientation and safety classes are followed by three days of intensive instruction on precisely how to be a welder, class II. Then Ken goes to work on the factory floor. Since his station comes early on the assembly line, he barely knows what a finished gadget looks like. And he knows next to nothing about the company's long-term plans.

The repetitive work is excruciatingly boring. Plant rules even dictate that Ken summon an electrician if a light bulb burns out. He finds that ridiculous. He knows, however, that if he performs satisfactorily as a welder, class II and sticks with it for a year, he can expect a raise and a promotion to welder, class I. The company is fair and honest about that. Still, Ken finds the work mind-numbing and dashes out the factory gate five minutes after quitting time. Greenville is a place to work, not a way of life.

The company is organized along extremely hierarchical lines. Indeed, Greenville Gadget Corporation is, in essence, a segregated society. Blue-collar and white-collar workers park in different lots, enter through different doors, eat in different cafeterias, and are paid on different bases (hourly versus monthly). The only managerial staff members Ken encounters frequently in his first year on the job are his foreman and the personnel manager who hired him.

At the factory, Ken works mostly by himself, like a machine. He is not expected to make suggestions for change, nor does he. Ken finds his foreman annoying: the man is constantly looking over his shoulder to see that everything is done by the book. The foreman, a former welder himself, doesn't like his job either. He occupies the awkward middle ground between "us" and "them" in the company and feels estranged from both sides.

There is one consolation: Ken is paid well. In fact, his hourly wage differs little from welders who have been on the job for years. He also gets generous health and life insurance benefits and a fine pension, though he does not expect to remain long enough to collect it. Nonetheless, he resents the much higher pay and generally better treatment accorded white-collar workers. Greenville's CEO, for example, earns 25 times as much as Ken and receives healthy stock options and profit-based incentive pay on top of that.

Like all blue-collar workers at Greenville, Ken belongs to the International Gadget Workers' Union. Union membership ends at the level of the foremen, who are viewed as part of management. Greenville and its union are locked into an adversarial relationship that is normally one of wary coexistence but occasionally breaks out into open hostility.

★★★

Across the Pacific, where Kenichi goes to work for Waseda Widget Works, things are starkly different. Waseda has not laid off a worker since the 1974 recession and dismisses only about one employee (out of 20,000) per year for cause. While there is no legal long-term commitment on either side, Kenichi expects to make a career at Waseda, and the company views him as a lifetime employee. Neither side expects Kenichi to seek a better job elsewhere, as prospects for mid-career job changes in Japan are poor.

There are no rigid job classifications at Waseda, so Kenichi is trained to perform a wide variety of tasks. Some of this training is done in the company school, which he attends for three weeks. There he learns not only about the technology behind the manufacture of widgets, but also about the use and sale of widgets and the history and philosophy of the company. However, most of the technical training takes place on the shop floor, where senior workers take responsibility for Kenichi's education as he rotates through every department in the factory. Kenichi never becomes as good a welder as Ken. But he does know how to paint, assemble, package, and inspect widgets.

Because work at Waseda is organized flexibly, Kenichi may find himself welding one week, painting the next, and so on. It all depends on what work needs to be done. If his machine malfunctions, Kenichi tries to fix it before calling an engineer. And he certainly changes light bulbs by himself! Kenichi likes the variety; it makes his work more interesting. He routinely stays past quitting time if his day's work is not done.

The environment at Waseda is much more egalitarian than at Greenville. Everyone, even the executives, wears the company uniform, eats in the same cafeteria, and is paid by the month. In the mornings, they do calisthenics together; after work, they go out to the same bars. Early in his career, Kenichi encounters young management trainees in overalls doing the same jobs as he. Later, these men will assume executive positions, but they are learning the business from the ground up. Kenichi likes that.

Work at the factory is organized into teams that work independently, with little managerial supervision, and are encouraged to take initiative. Toward this end, they meet daily in quality circles. Kenichi feels that management cares about what he thinks, and he freely volunteers both information and ideas. Not infrequently, those suggestions lead to changes in the way his own work is done.

Pay at Waseda is determined largely by seniority, and seniority differentials are much larger than at Greenville. So Kenichi's starting salary is lower than Ken's. However, if they stay on the job for 10 years (which Kenichi will, but Ken will not), Kenichi will earn more. Pay differentials other than for seniority are, however, smaller at Waseda. Although managers do earn more than blue-collar workers, the pay gaps are much smaller than at Greenville. The CEO of Waseda, for example, receives a salary only 12 times as large as Kenichi's—and does not get the stock options and incentives that are the rule at Greenville.

Waseda practices holistic labor relations and does not draw a sharp line between the world of work and the world beyond. Kenichi lives in a company-provided apartment, gets his health care at the company hospital, and plays baseball on Sundays at the company's recre-

"Even if I can't lift your shipment,
I can still pick it up."

Kin Wong
Courier, Taipei, Taiwan

At Federal Express, we'll pick up and deliver big shipments as well as small ones.
In fact, when it comes to international air freight, we carry more weight than anyone in the
industry. Something which should give a big lift to shippers everywhere.

ational facility. He occasionally vacations at the company's resort on Guam. To him, Waseda is like an extended family. He seeks advice from his boss about marriage and educating his children and expects company executives to attend his father's funeral.

At Waseda, all employees except top managers belong to the Waseda Widget Employees' Union. The union sees itself as part of the company, not as an adversary of management. Indeed, most managers began their careers as union members. Company executives routinely consult the union on all major decisions. There has not been a strike in recent memory.

★★★

Now, who would you rather be, Ken or Kenichi? No, that's the wrong question. Kenichi lives in cramped quarters in a crowded country where conformism is the rule and individualism is frowned upon. Almost all Americans would rather live in New York City than in Tokyo, in Youngstown than in Nagoya. The right question is whether Ken would be more productive if he were treated like Kenichi on the job. There are reasons to think he would. One is that Japanese transplants use these techniques successfully on American soil with American workers. Another is that a number of leading American companies have long practiced elements of Japanese-style labor relations. Let us consider in greater detail what we know about the key differences between the two systems.

1. *Job Security.* Lifetime employment is central to the Japanese way of doing business. Workers whose jobs are secure are not threatened by change. Like Robert Hubble, they welcome innovations that are good for the company. That is precisely why the Japan Productivity Center made job security one of its three guiding principles when it began its productivity-enhancement campaign in 1955.

Critics often point out, correctly, that only a minority of Japanese workers are on lifetime employment. Some go on to claim that Japanese workers as a group enjoy no more job security than American workers. The allegation is that industrial giants like Toyota and Matsushita get their subcontractors and suppliers to act as shock absorbers by laying off their workers during business downturns so the big companies do not have to lay off theirs. But the allegation is at best a half-truth. Yes, large Japanese firms do offer more stable employment than small ones, but that is also true in the United States. The most amazing comparative statistic I have come across is this: The typical employee of a Japanese company with less than 10 workers has been on the job as long as the typical employee of an American firm with more than 1,000 employees. Loosely speaking, the corner drugstore in Tokyo offers its workers as much job security as General Motors.

Many American firms treat their employees—in the words of one executive—"just like a box of Kleenex: if one left, another would pop up." Japanese firms, by contrast, treat their employees more like part of the family. A significant number of American companies do, of course, offer Japanese-style job security. Most of these are industrial giants like IBM and Hewlett-Packard. But there are examples of small companies in which lifetime employment works well.

Hugh Aaron headed a plastics company with just 100 employees. He found laying off workers not only distasteful but costly, since he frequently lost valuable employees who did not wait around to be recalled. So he proposed a deal to his employees: He would end layoffs if they would work overtime when necessary and perform any reasonable job request. Employees accepted eagerly, and according to Aaron "it worked marvelously. Employee morale attained a new height. . . . We had, in a sense, become a stable, cohesive 'family.'" The firm, which was sold eight years later, never had another layoff.

While lifetime employment is not the only difference between labor-management relations in the U.S. and Japan, it is the centerpiece. It leads directly, for example, to the next distinction.

2. *Training.* Japanese firms invest much more in training their workers. While American companies typically spend between 1 percent and 2 percent of payroll on training programs, Japanese companies spend about double that. When Japanese companies come here, they bring their high-training strategy with them. A 1987 study found that Japanese transplants in the U.S. spend about two and a half times as much on training as their American counterparts. An MIT study of the automobile industry unearthed an even starker difference: Japanese auto plants in North America give their workers about eight times as much training as U.S. plants. A series of interviews I conducted with executives of multinationals that operate in both the U.S. and Japan indicated that Japanese companies provide more training than American companies, whichever country they operate in.

This difference in training appears to be part of a broad personnel strategy that works only because Japanese companies expect their workers to stay with them for the long haul.

3. *Job Rotation and Flexibility.* Extensive training and job rotation not only give the Japanese firm a highly skilled work force, they also give it an extremely flexible one. That, in turn, makes it much easier to respond to changes in demand and technology—and to guarantee lifetime employment, as Hugh Aaron's plastics company illustrates. It also yields productivity fruits.

Marvin Runyon, a former Ford executive who established Nissan's first assembly plant in the United States, once said he could accomplish at Ford what he did at Nissan "if you promise me I won't have unreasonable union work rules." He used a light bulb in the Nissan

"Participative management does not mean permissive management," said Marvin Runyon, president of Nissan in 1982. "It means worker input is requested, wanted, and used."

factory ceiling to illustrate. "If I have to change that bulb, I might get a ladder and do it myself or call one of the custodians. If this were Ford, I would have to have an electrician change the bulb and someone else carry the ladder." This is but one trivial example of a broader phenomenon: human beings have the capacity to reason and react to a wide variety of unforeseen circumstances—if they are given the discretion to do so. But if instead they are treated like automatons, they will do no better than machines.

4. *Egalitarian Workplaces.* Japan prides itself on having created a classless corporate community. This is no doubt an exaggeration in a society in which no one ever forgets his station in life. A Japanese business is no Athenian democracy; all that bowing signifies something. Nonetheless, the typical Japanese workplace has much less of what I call "in your face" privilege than its American counterpart.

Here's a homely example of behavior that is virtually unthinkable in a Japanese company. About a year ago, I visited a top executive of a leading retail firm in New York City—a bright and friendly man. To reach his office on the eighth floor above a large store, I had to ride the executive elevator. When it stopped on the third floor, a sales clerk tried to board, but the elevator man haughtily refused her entry with the words, "This is the executive elevator." You could tell from the look in her eyes and the protest in her voice that her next customer might not get the courteous, efficient service on which the store prides itself. And what did the company gain from this little exercise of privilege?

A little consideration for employees can go a long way. Shortly after Victor Kiam bought Remington Products in Bridgeport, Connecticut, he shook hands with the man who swept the parking lot and told him he was doing a great job. It is said that the lot has remained the cleanest in New England ever since. And it didn't cost Remington a dime.

5. *Teamwork and Participation.* Japanese normally work in teams. Quality circles—an American invention—are extensive and successful. The Japan Productivity Center estimates that about 85 percent of all employees of major Japanese manufacturing companies take part in a quality circle and that the average worker makes 22 suggestions per year! From a geyser of ideas like that, a few good ones are bound to spew forth now and then.

But employee involvement in Japan extends well beyond quality circles. It includes formal joint consultations between labor and management on virtually all major corporate decisions, including those usually thought to be the prerogatives of management. The process can be ponderous and agonizingly slow. But once a consensual decision is made, the whole organization snaps to.

The Japanese hold no patent on teamwork. In the mid–1980s, IBM's personal-computer division found it could save money by purchasing circuit boards from an external supplier rather than manufacturing them at its factory in Austin, Texas. Because of its lifetime-employment policy, however, IBM did not want to close the plant. So it gave plant managers a chance to cut costs first. Local managers responded by reorganizing work into teams, each of which performed a variety of tasks. They broadened both job classifications and the responsibilities of each employee. It worked. By 1990, productivity had tripled, quality was five times better, and the plant's employment had grown.

One woman, who has worked in the factory since 1969, symbolizes the changes. Before the reorganization, she fed circuit boards into a machine—one by one, about 1,200 each day—and removed them when the machine finished its work. She now tends the machine only about a quarter of her day. The rest of the time she deals with suppliers and customers, keeps quality records, helps decide on equipment purchases for the plant, and meets daily for discussions with her work team. "I've been working a lot harder," she says, "but it's worth it."

6. *Pay Structures and Fringe Benefits.* A number of studies have compared wage structures in the U.S. and Japan. All conclude that wage differentials other than for seniority are smaller in Japan, but the financial reward for longevity in the firm is much greater. No one should be surprised that such a wage structure encourages workers to stay on the job longer.

Contrary to legend, however, profit-sharing is not common in Japan. Most workers do receive sizable bonuses in June and December. But those bonuses are mainly deferred wage payments that come, conveniently, at gift-giving seasons—sort of like Christmas clubs. They depend little, if at all, on the firm's profits.

Fringe benefits at big Japanese companies, however, are truly impressive. Large firms in the United States offer their employees extensive fringes, but these are nothing compared to standard practice in Japan. There, employees of major companies often receive free (or highly subsidized) housing, food and drink on the company, medical care at company clinics and hospitals, vacations in company resorts, company-provided banking services, and more. The company is, indeed, a way of life.

All and all, the frequently drawn analogy between a Japanese firm and an extended family does not seem too farfetched. The key question, of course, is whether these highly paternalistic labor practices can be profitably imported to the United States, where both workers and managers come from such a different culture. Corning apparently thinks many of them can. So do leading companies like

Hewlett-Packard, which exported some of those very practices to Japan years ago. So does General Motors, which used the lessons it learned from Toyota at their jointly owned plant in Fremont, California, to create its unconventional Saturn division. So, most obviously, do Honda, Toyota, Nissan, and other successful Japanese transplants in the U.S. And so do I.

Bowing, wearing the company uniform or lapel pin, and drinking with the boss after work may be inappropriate in the American setting. Nor would we want to emulate the darker side of the Japanese system—like rigid conformism and outrageous sex discrimination. But some aspects of Japanese labor relations have universal appeal. Surely American workers crave job security, prefer variety over routinized boredom, would like to be consulted about how their workplaces are organized, and have a yen to share in their companies' good fortunes, just like their Japanese counterparts.

When the Japan Productivity Center organized its remarkably successful productivity-enhancement campaign in 1955, it was worried about how workers would cope with and react to rapid technological change. To meet this challenge, it suggested that Japanese firms adopt three guiding principles:

• *Job Security* so that workers would not fear losing their jobs when modern technology sent productivity soaring.

• *Joint Consultation* between labor and management so that workers had a voice in how their enterprises were run.

• *Fair Sharing* of the gains from productivity growth to promote solidarity and cooperation.

That was Japan in 1955. This is America in 1991. But the principles that worked there and then seem just as appropriate here and now. They would be fine principles for an American productivity-enhancement campaign. And the sooner we get started, the better.

In the American context, the first principle probably translates into the bargain summarized by Marvin Runyon: firms pledge job security for workers in return for flexibility in the workplace. Such a trade should appeal to both sides. After all, it is difficult to see what union workers find attractive about narrow job descriptions and restrictive work practices—except that they protect specific jobs. And firms would be in a better position to guarantee job security if they had more freedom to move workers around.

The second principle leads most naturally to worker participation. Workers need to feel that their opinions are solicited and respected. They are, after all, not robots. And companies might gain a great deal from the suggestions their employees could make.

The third principle may be the most contentious. A knee-jerk reaction might be to criticize it as vaguely socialistic. Not so. In the

American context, it would probably mean two things. First, more profit-sharing, which, I have argued, may well bring productivity dividends. Second, a narrowing of the extraordinary pay-and-privilege gap between ordinary workers and top executives, which is probably greater here than anywhere else on earth. This last may well prove unpopular in the executive suite.

All these things and more can be done by American management right now. No enabling legislation is required. No huge capital expenditures stand in the way. Japan has already provided a set of blueprints that can be adapted to our circumstances. As soon as the will is found, the way will be clear.

"Using Federal Express to distribute Sharp® parts was a sharp idea."

Conrad Westerman
Federal Express Warehouse Manager, Memphis

Recently, Sharp Electronics started using our Memphis-based Business Logistics Services
division for the storage and distribution of important office
equipment parts. And quickly discovered that they could cut both warehousing
costs. *And* delivery time. Quite sharply.

CHAPTER 6

THE PUBLIC'S CAPITAL

One day in the early 1980s, I spoke at a business conference along with Amitai Etzioni, the noted sociologist. As I awaited my turn to speak, I listened to Etzioni talk of togetherness, or rather its lack, in contemporary American society. His catalog of unmet collective needs included our inadequate public infrastructure, and he concluded with a remark that struck me as hilarious at the time: "On your way home, if you come to a bridge, don't cross it."

Not long afterward, a portion of the bridge over the Mianus River on the Connecticut Turnpike—a bridge I had often crossed—collapsed. The remark no longer seemed so funny. Within the next few years, a number of other not-very-funny incidents occurred: a New York State Thruway bridge collapsed, killing 10 motorists; a dam burst in Georgia, flooding a Bible school and drowning a number of children; and so on.

Tragedies like those helped focus public attention on America's crumbling infrastructure. But they were also misleading. Only a morbid individual worries about drowning from a collapsing bridge or a bursting dam. But all of us deal frequently with more mundane hazards like being stuck in traffic jams, jarred by pothole-ridden roads, or delayed at crowded airports. Many of us also worry about the quality of our municipal water supplies. In a sense less dramatic than the bridge over the Mianus River, public health, safety, and convenience—and national productivity—are imperiled by the way America starves its public sector.

Contrary to a recent cliché, we have no infrastructure *crisis*. We are not on the verge of a cataclysm nor at a dramatic historical crossroads. But we do have a nagging infrastructure *problem*. America's bumpy roads, teetering and sometimes closed bridges, and congested airports symbolize a seriously deteriorating public capital stock. Fifteen years of policy aimed at boosting private investment and stinting on public investment has left America with what has aptly been called a third deficit—a serious imbalance between relatively abundant private capital and relatively scarce public capital. And we have no one to blame but ourselves.

The third deficit is sizable, as are its ill effects. A few years ago, the Federal Highway Administration estimated that 53 percent of nonlocal roads were in fair or poor condition. Substandard road surfaces cost Americans upward of $30 billion a year in vehicle damage and excess fuel consumption alone; no one knows how to put a price tag on the aches and pains and annoyance. Across the nation about 136,000 bridges are rated structurally deficient. The estimated bill for bringing them all up to par exceeds $50 billion.

Roughly half of all urban interstates and a third of other urban arterial highways are congested, making traffic jams a shared ritual of modern American life. During the 1980s, commuting delays into Manhattan doubled, and rush-hour driving speeds on the Washington, D.C., beltway fell by 15 to 50 percent. The U.S. Department of Transportation (DOT) estimated that 722 million person-hours and three billion gallons of gasoline were wasted in urban freeway delays in 1985. The total cost of this congestion: about $9 billion. And things keep getting worse.

The nation's airports are also choked with traffic. No wonder. While air traffic has risen about 9 percent a year, the nation has not opened a single major airport since 1974. (Denver is building one now.) According to the DOT, all 21 of the nation's primary airports, which together handle 80 percent of the traffic, are seriously congested. The Federal Aviation Administration estimated that in 1986 air-travel delays cost airlines $1.8 billion in additional operating expenses and cost travelers $3.2 billion in lost time.

All this does not constitute a crisis. But it is certainly a colossal waste. The total cost may run to $50 billion or more a year. More to the point of this book, America's shortage of infrastructure capital may also be retarding productivity growth. By one estimate, it accounts for more than half of the total productivity slowdown since the early 1970s. This estimate, produced by economist David Aschauer, is quite controversial. So we should pause a moment to understand precisely what it means and just how stunning it is.

According to Aschauer's research, the slowdown in the rate of investment in *public* capital was a major cause of the slowdown in *private-sector* productivity growth. The implication is clear: If the government would invest more in core infrastructure—roads and bridges, water and sewer systems, airports and mass transit, electrical and gas facilities—productivity growth would accelerate. At one level this conclusion is unremarkable. I have observed several times in this book that workers with more capital are more productive. Why should public capital be different from private capital in this respect?

Just as a truck driver can produce more work per hour if his truck is bigger and more reliable, so can he be more productive if the roads are smoother and less congested—not to mention passable.

Why, then, has Aschauer's work ignited a tempest in the Washington think-tank teapot? Because his estimates of the productivity-enhancing effects of public capital are so large that many people refuse to believe them. They imply, for example, that productivity growth since 1970 would have been 50 percent higher if we had held the rate of public investment (relative to GNP) at 1950-1970 levels. They also imply that public investment would now contribute more to private-sector productivity growth than private investment—as anti-Reaganesque a conclusion as you are likely to encounter.

Critics have attacked Aschauer's work on a variety of technical grounds, and others have scurried to its defense. This is not the place to join the technical debate. Perhaps his estimates are too high. But all the fuss seems to have missed an obvious and fundamental point. The conclusion that the nation should invest more in infrastructure may well be right even if Aschauer's estimates of the productivity impacts are wrong. Why? Because many, if not most, of the benefits from public-infrastructure capital do not even count in the GNP.

Some years ago, my wife and I bumped into an example. We were driving home late at night from a lovely restaurant on the Pennsylvania side of the Delaware River when our car, which was new at the time, hit what must have been one of history's great potholes. It was new no longer. The resulting impact not only flattened a tire and ruined our evening but bent two wheels out of shape and destroyed the front-end suspension. Had Pennsylvania better maintained its public infrastructure, the Blinder family would have benefited. But the GNP would not have recorded our gain. In fact, GNP would have been smaller because we would have spent less on auto repairs.

Now suppose I had been a truck driver returning from a delivery. Because of the time spent changing the flat, my delivery might have taken four hours instead of two. Pennsylvania's shoddy infrastructure would have reduced my productivity (GNP per hour of work), and therefore better infrastructure would have boosted GNP.

The general point is clear: smoother road surfaces lead to less maintenance and faster travel not only for trucks on business trips but also for cars in personal use. But while the former are reckoned into the GNP, where they appear as productivity improvements, the latter are not. (In fact, they may actually lower the GNP, as my example suggests.) And other benefits of better roads—like the fact that people with backache suffer less pain—do not affect the productivity statistics at all. The only benefits that enter into Aschauer's calculations of the worth of public capital are the ones that boost GNP. So his calculations miss much of consequence.

The same point applies to infrastructure investments that alleviate congestion. If expanded highway and airport capacity enables truckers and pilots to accomplish more work in an hour, productivity will rise. That is precisely what Aschauer measures—and what his critics dispute. But if families on vacation endure fewer traffic jams and airport delays, or if millions of commuters cut minutes from their morning drive times, the GNP statistics will record no gain.

The upshot: Aschauer's estimate that public capital is more productive than private capital is astonishing—once you realize how much it leaves out. Only some of the returns on public capital actually get counted in GNP. That these alone might exceed the total returns on private capital is truly remarkable. Even if Aschauer overstates the effects of infrastructure on GNP by a factor of two, the nation might still be well advised to start pouring cement.

Or would it? There is at least one important reason to question this conclusion. And it has major implication for the debate over infrastructure and productivity.

MAKING SOMETHING FROM NOTHING

What the nation really wants and needs is not more roads, bridges, and airports but more trucks, cars, and aircraft carrying more passengers and freight more smoothly, conveniently, and in less time. Building additional physical facilities is the most obvious way to achieve that goal. But it is not the only way. And it is a very expensive way. Advocates of greater infrastructure spending have bandied about figures on "unmet needs" that run as high as $2 trillion and more. That is a titanic sum—enough to sink several budgets. Not only that, the solution sows the seeds of its own destruction because, for example, more roads will surely attract more drivers to damage and crowd the greater volume of pavement.

Fortunately, a team of economists has recently proposed two more subtle and less costly means to the same end. Instead of building more highways, Kenneth Small, Clifford Winston, and Carol Evans argue, we should make better use of the ones we've got. Build our roads better and charge more intelligently for their use, they claim, and the American public will get more and better highway services at lower cost. Let us see how.

To start, the trio finds that current building practice makes roads too thin, so they begin crumbling too soon. Building roadways to last longer costs more initially but yields substantial savings in maintenance and repair costs later. The economists estimate that thicker pavement—for example, about two more inches on interstates— would eventually save taxpayers at least $4 for every $1 of public expenditure, including interest. Even if their calculations err by a considerable margin, this simple change in policy has much to recommend it. Other experts point out that rubberized asphalt—created by adding rubber from old tires to asphalt—lasts longer and decreases vehicle wear and tear.

But what about pricing? Elementary economic principles suggest that the fee each vehicle pays for road use ought to approximate the costs that vehicle imposes on society. There are two principal costs: damage to the roadway and congestion. Loosely speaking, trucks cause the damage and cars cause the congestion. So each requires a different approach.

Trucks pay considerable road-use taxes, as we all know. Indeed, they must be the only pieces of capital that wear their tax bills on their rear ends. Unfortunately, taxes on trucks ignore important engineering evidence that the damage a vehicle does to a roadway depends not on its total weight but on its weight per axle. This is, after all, just common sense. (Or is it common physics?) The weight of a truck is not distributed evenly over the road but concentrated at points where tire meets pavement. Distributing the same weight over more points (more axles) eases the strain on the pavement. So we should encourage the use of trucks with many axles.

Yet what do we do now? First, we charge for road use principally through a gasoline tax that actually penalizes multi-axle trucks, which are generally larger and less fuel-efficient. Then we levy a special excise tax on tires, so multiwheeled vehicles pay more. Finally, many toll roads charge by the axle—precisely the reverse of what they should be doing. If road-use fees were based on vehicle weight per axle, America's truck fleet would be redesigned in ways that do less damage to both our roads and our pocketbooks.

With cars, the principal concern is congestion, not road damage. When Joe Commuter decides to drive to work rather than take the train, he presumably takes account of the traffic delays he will encounter on the road. But he ignores the fact that his decision to drive slows down the progress of every other driver on the congested roads. Because Joe does not weigh the full *social* costs of his decision, he drives too much and at the wrong hours.

The economic remedy is simple in principle, and modern technology makes it much more practical than it once was: drivers should pay more for using roads during rush hours than during slack periods. The gasoline tax makes a slight nod in this direction, because fuel economy declines in heavy traffic. But economists who have studied the matter conclude that charges for road use in peak periods should be much higher than they are now. With more appropriate pricing, traffic would spread itself out more evenly over the day, and the existing road network would accommodate more cars traveling at higher speeds.

The same principles apply to our overcrowded airports, where pricing can only be called wacky. Airport landing fees generally depend on weight. But the main cost of accommodating an additional plane at a busy airport is not the damage it does to the runway but the delays it imposes on other aircraft. Thus, while a tiny Beechcraft costs society about as much to land as a Boeing 747, airports charge it much less. And even though it costs vastly more to handle any plane at 6 p.m. than at 1 p.m., landing fees rarely vary by time of day.

Rational airport pricing would make landing fees depend on time of day rather than on aircraft weight. If airport services were priced this way, much general aviation traffic would voluntarily divert itself to smaller reliever airports rather than land at Kennedy, O'Hare, and LAX. Commercial airlines would spread their traffic out more evenly through the day. Delays would shorten and the nation would suddenly find its existing airports able to handle more traffic. It would be as if we got something for nothing. Correction: We *would* have gotten something for nothing.

Some people have used the preceding analysis to argue that we should not build any more infrastructure; instead, we should utilize what we have more efficiently. This conclusion seems to me illogical. We should always use whatever resources we have more efficiently. But that does not preclude building more. There are at least four reasons why I believe America should invest more in its roads, bridges, airports, and water-treatment facilities.

The first is their apparently dramatic effect on national productivity. It is true that the nation could—and should—get more out of the capital already on hand. But if such large benefits flow from such inefficiently used infrastructure, there is a strong presumption that efficiently used infrastructure would offer real bonanzas.

Second, the share of infrastructure spending has declined from about 2 percent of GNP in the 1960s to about 1 percent in the 1980s, which suggests underinvestment. Critics of greater infrastructure spending point out that real GNP has grown about 70 percent in two decades; so 1 percent of today's GNP buys almost as much as 2 percent of GNP did then. But we must remember that economically speaking America is now a much bigger place. There are, for example, 23 percent more Americans living now than 20 years ago, about half again as many cars and trucks on the road, and about twice as many aircraft in the skies. Why should we think that the 1970 absolute spending levels are appropriate today?

Third, America has accumulated private capital much more rapidly than public capital for several decades now, making private capital relatively more abundant and public capital relatively more scarce. According to the so-called (and widely misunderstood) law of diminishing returns, this dramatic shift in relative supplies should have raised the productivity of public capital compared with that of private capital. So there are two possibilities: Either the productivity of public capital was exceedingly low in 1970, or it is exceedingly high today. You choose.

Fourth, when given a choice at the ballot box, Americans vote overwhelmingly in favor of more infrastructure spending. Despite the vaunted tax revolt, voters in the 1980s approved more than three-quarters of all bond referenda for infrastructure. And the typical outcome was lopsided—about a two-to-one margin in favor. The message seems clear: Americans are willing to tax themselves to build roads, bridges, sewage-treatment plants, and the like. Maybe they know what they're doing.

WHOSE PROBLEM IS IT?

Careless discussions of the infrastructure shortage often proceed as if it were all a federal problem. It is not. A large portion of the nation's infrastructure is, in fact, the responsibility of state and local governments, and the conditions of highways and bridges vary enormously across the 50 states.

The Federal Highway Administration estimates that 13 percent of all the deficient bridges covered by the federal aid system are in a single state: New York. More than 54 percent of the Empire State's bridges that receive federal aid are deficient, while just across the river (if you can get across a bridge), New Jersey's deficiency rate is only 21 percent. New York and New Jersey receive federal aid according to the same formulas, have similar weather, and buy concrete at similar prices. The difference presumably reflects New Jersey's superior performance on bridge repair.

Even larger discrepancies exist in road conditions. Whereas about 12 percent of the interstate highway system was in poor condition at the end of 1987, the figure was a stunning 40 percent in Missouri but less than 5 percent in neighboring Illinois and 1 percent or less in eight particularly tidy states. Again, the suspicion is that different state maintenance policies are at the bottom of this.

That a good part of the infrastructure problem has its roots at state and local levels does not preclude a federal role. State and local governments respond to both political and economic incentives. And the economic incentives, at least, are heavily influenced by federal matching grants that lower the price of infrastructure for states. If the federal government offers to match state expenditures on a three-for-one basis, for example, a $40 million span of highway will cost the state that builds it just $10 million. The other $30 million comes from Washington. Economists have found, not surprisingly, that such incentives encourage more construction. There are two problems, however.

One is that federal grant programs are typically capped, and spending in many states is at or beyond the cap. In such cases, the state becomes ineligible for further federal aid, and the inducement to spend more disappears. The remedy, of course, is to uncap the programs. But Congress is naturally worried about open-ended commitments. Perhaps a good solution, recently suggested by a group of congressmen, is to lower the matching rate but eliminate the caps.

The second problem is more worrisome. Nowadays many of our most acute infrastructure needs are for maintaining and repairing existing roads and bridges, not for building new ones. The interstate highway system, for example, is nearly complete; but parts of it are in sorry shape. Unfortunately, state and local politicians who send road crews out to repair potholes and reinforce bridges earn no photo opportunities, cut no ribbons, and get no sound bites on the TV news. But when local politicians announce plans for a new bridge, the local media lavish attention and compliment them on their ability to pry money out of Washington.

Such political incentives produce what has been called an edifice complex—a bias in favor of building new rather than fixing up. This bias was not created by the federal government. But if Washington ignores it, the nation may develop an ever-increasing imbalance in its stock of public infrastructure. One thing we certainly do *not* need is more and more decrepit bridges. What to do? One idea is for the federal government to provide more generous matching grants for maintenance and repairs and less generous ones for new construction.

★★★

If public investment is to live up to its potential as a source of productivity growth, it is imperative to get the incentives right. State and local governments must be given appropriate incentives to build the right types of capital, and individuals and businesses must be given appropriate incentives to utilize infrastructure efficiently. In addition to all this, however, we probably need to build more.

And public infrastructure has a final virtue—one I have not yet mentioned but that bears on a central theme of this book. Unlike a private home, office building, or factory, a publicly owned bridge, road, or airport is neither mine nor yours. It is everybody's. We own it together. Upgrading our shabby stock of infrastructure will contribute to the sense of social cohesion and even of togetherness that we need to take to other spheres of life—like the workplace.

"I help Delacre cookies batter the competition."

Doug Hottel
Worldwide Account Executive, Brussels, Belgium

For the Campbell Soup Company and its Belgian subsidiary, Biscuits Delacre,
Federal Express is an essential ingredient in their pan-European marketing recipe.
Delacre uses Federal Express international delivery service to ship new products from
Belgium for testing at Campbell's research center in the U.S. which enables them to
cut product development time. And deliver their cookies to market faster.
A competitive advantage that can be particularly sweet.

GROWING TOGETHER

f one man symbolized the failed growth strategy of the 1980s, it was neither junk-bond artist Michael Milken nor buyout king Henry Kravis. It was Wrong Way Corrigan, the flier who in 1938 took off from New York's Floyd Bennett Field bound for California but who landed in Ireland. Where did the growth strategy of the 1980s go wrong? The simple answer is *everywhere*. It flew off in the wrong direction.

• Reaganomics began with the premise that government is an obstacle to growth, a nuisance that must be cleared away like underbrush. There is a dash of truth here. Excessive taxation and oppressive regulation surely dampen the spirit of capitalist enterprise.

But I have argued that government should do much more than just get out of the way. It can and should care for society's underdogs, and especially for their children, so the next generation grows up augmenting rather than depleting the national treasure. It can and should better educate the nation's youth so that every American is literate and numerate, so the vast majority are high-school graduates, and so at least a few more opt for careers in science. It can and should build more public infrastructure to facilitate commerce, improve the quality of life, and raise productivity.

• The Reagan program stressed incentives, as is proper. But supply-siders took an exceedingly narrow view of the matter, portraying lower taxes as the main, if not the only, route to faster growth. Author George Gilder, the poet laureate of the movement, was blunter than most when he wrote, "To help the poor and middle classes, one must cut the tax rates of the rich"—a sentiment whose callousness is exceeded only by its naiveté.

The growth program offered here emphasizes incentives too, but not in the form of tax cuts. Workers may be better motivated and more productive if they have a stake in their companies' profits and are consulted on how to do their jobs. Children at risk may perform better in school if they are adequately nourished, receive decent medical care, and attend a quality preschool. Appropriate incentives would get state and local governments providing the right kinds of infrastructure and households and businesses utilizing those precious assets more efficiently. Incentives all. But none of them are tax cuts, and none would widen the gap between rich and poor.

• Reaganites saw private capital formation as the fulcrum of growth and advocated hefty tax breaks for savers and investors. President Bush continues this tradition with his vain and by now halfhearted attempt to reinstate a preferentially low tax rate for capital gains.

More rapid accumulation of business capital would be welcome, of course. But I have argued that using artificial tax inducements to achieve this end may do more harm than good. Furthermore, computers and generators—not to mention racehorses—are not the only productive forms of capital. Other types of investment—in children at risk, in training our work force, and in public infrastructure—offer even higher returns.

• Finally, the growth strategy of the 1980s glorified a swaggering, John Wayne form of capitalism aptly captured by former trade negotiator Clyde Prestowitz's metaphor of the cowboy "rolling back the frontier, laying the trails, marking the water holes, and moving on." As Prestowitz suggests, a more durable industrial strategy may require more of the spirit of the pioneers who settled the American West. "Settlers are seldom glamorous. They dress like hicks, worry a lot, and are never fast on the draw. But in the hundreds they come, and they stick together. Hampered by children and oxen and Grandma, they don't travel fast, but they do move inexorably west. By working together. By fixing wagon wheels—together. By raising barns—together. By starting towns—together."

Togetherness is a corny idea whose time may have come back. With more settlers and fewer cowboys in the 1980s, America might have displayed more concern for the common good and invested more in the future. We would have educated our youth better and built more public facilities. And we would never have permitted the lowest 20 percent of the group to fall by the wayside, because "they" would have been seen as part of "us." Perhaps the 1990s will be different.

American productivity has barely crawled upward these past two decades—roughly 1¼ percent per annum. The growth dividends promised by Reaganomics never materialized. Real wages and standards of living have stagnated. Income disparities and economic class distinctions have widened. The strategy of piling on debt, so seductive while the party lasted, left us with a workout of Brobdingnagian proportions. Many despair that America can do little to improve upon its miserable recent growth record. Some say we must content ourselves with less.

The message of this book is neither contentment nor resignation. Rather, it is that we should raise our sights and, unlike Wrong Way Corrigan, change course—toward a human-resource-based growth strategy that percolates up from the bottom and middle rather than trickles down from the top. Will we do it? That is not for me to say, for the answer depends more on the vagaries of politics than on the force of economic logic. According to some seers, American politics is on the verge of another big political sea change. Republican political theorist Kevin Phillips, for example, believes "that the 1990s [will] be a time in which to correct the excesses of the 1980s." Why? Because "the dangers posed by excessive individualism, greed, and insufficient concern for America as a community went beyond the issue of fairness," he says, and set the political stage for reform.

Is Phillips right? Don't ask me. My failings as a political forecaster are matched only by my inability to predict the National League pennant winner. My purpose is not to forecast America's future but to point out that there are wiser counsels than the counsel of despair. We have options. There are policies we can implement that stand a real chance of improving America's growth performance.

None of the policies advocated here are foolproof. None will double or triple the productivity growth rate. But that is asking too much. Remember that the Japanese came roaring into the late 20th century by maintaining a growth differential over the U.S. of just three-quarters of a percentage point. Raising America's productivity growth rate by three-quarters of a percentage point is a worthy goal. And it is within the realm of the possible, if we set our sights high and work together.

"We didn't just start an air express service. We started a revolution."

At Federal Express, we do a lot more than deliver packages and freight swiftly and dependably to more than 120 countries worldwide. We work in partnership with companies to design and operate the most sophisticated business logistics systems in the world. This allows companies to expand their markets, improve productivity, and compete more efficiently in a rapidly-changing global economy. You could call it revolutionary.

NOTES ON SOURCES

CHAPTER 1

Much of the information on comparative and historical growth rates is artfully compiled by William J. Baumol, Sue Anne Batey Blackman, and Edward N. Wolff in *Productivity and American Leadership: The Long View* (The MIT Press, 1989).

CHAPTER 2

The Adam Smith quotation is from *The Wealth of Nations*, Modern Library Edition (New York: Random House, 1937), p. 423. Data on saving and investment come from *Economic Report of the President, 1991* and the Federal Reserve Bank of New York. Data on family income and income inequality are from U.S. Bureau of the Census, *Current Population Reports*, Series P-60, No. 168 (September 1990). I use data that are deflated by the experimental CPI rather than the official CPI, because the latter exaggerated inflation in the 1970s (which is why the CPI was revised in 1983). Data on the distribution of taxes are Congressional Budget Office estimates reported in the *1990 Green Book* of the House Ways and Means Committee (U.S. Government Printing Office, June 1990).

CHAPTER 3

The estimates of effective tax rates under ACRS are from Don Fullerton and Yolanda K. Henderson's "Incentive Effects of Taxes on Income From Capital: Alternative Policies in the 1980s," in *The Legacy of Reaganomics*, Charles R. Hulten and

Isabel V. Sawhill, editors (Washington, D.C.: The Urban Institute Press, 1984). Data on saving and investment are from *Economic Report of the President, 1991*. George Mitchell was quoted in *The Washington Post*, April 10, 1986. My own book, referred to in this chapter, is *Hard Heads, Soft Hearts* (Reading, Mass.: Addison-Wesley, 1987).

CHAPTER 4

The CED report is *Children In Need: Investment Strategies for the Educationally Disadvantaged* (CED: New York, 1987). It is updated in *The Unfinished Agenda: A New Vision for Child Development and Education* (CED: New York, 1991). Many of the findings on pre- and postnatal care are summarized in *Opportunities for Success: Cost Effective Programs for Children (Update 1988)*, a report of the Select Committee on Children, Youth and Families, U.S. House of Representatives, 100th Cong., 2d Session, 1988. The Harlem experiment is described in *As the Twig is Bent: Lasting Effects of Preschool Programs* (Hillsdale, New Jersey: Lawrence Erlbaum Associates, 1983). The follow-up study to Harlem Head Start is discussed in the CED report *Investing in Our Children: Business and the Public Schools* (CED: New York, 1985). Lester Thurow's description of foreign and American factories appears in his book *The Zero-Sum Solution: Building a World-Class American Economy* (New York: Simon & Schuster, 1985). The Perry program is described and evaluated in John R. Berrueta-Clement, et al., *Changed Lives:*

The Effects of the Perry Preschool Program on Youths Through Age 19 (Ypsilanti, Mich.: The High/Scope Press, 1984).

CHAPTER 5

The NEC story comes from Shintaro Ishihara's *The Japan That Can Say No* (Simon & Schuster, 1991). William Ouchi's *Theory Z: How American Business Can Meet the Japanese Challenge* was published by Addison-Wesley in 1981. Martin L. Weitzman's book is *The Share Economy: Conquering Stagflation* (Harvard University Press, 1984). The evidence alluded to on profit-sharing and worker participation can be found in *Paying for Productivity: A Look at the Evidence*, Alan S. Blinder, editor (Washington, D.C.: Brookings, 1990); the quotation from Weitzman and Kruse appears on p. 100. The story and quotations about Corning's labor practices come from John Hoerr's article "Sharpening Minds for a Competitive Edge," *Business Week*, December 17, 1990, pp. 72-78. Ray Schultz described the Hampton Inn program in his article "Satisfaction Guaranteed for Customers and Crew," *The Wall Street Journal*, January 28, 1991. Much of the information on Japanese labor practices is based on Alan S. Blinder and Alan B. Krueger's "International Differences in Labor Turnover: A Comparative Study with Emphasis on the U.S. and Japan," a paper prepared for the project on Time Horizons of American Industry sponsored by the Council on Competitiveness and the Harvard Business School. Hugh Aaron told his story in his article "Recession-Proofing a Company's Employees," *The Wall Street Journal*, March 4, 1991, p. A8. The quotation about Kleenex and the story about Victor Kiam both come from *The Economist*, March 2, 1991, p. 64. Marvin Runyon is quoted by Clyde V. Prestowitz Jr. in *Trading Places: How We Allowed Japan to Take the Lead* (New York: Basic Books, 1988), p. 212. The story about IBM's Austin plant comes from Nan Stone's article

"Does Business Have any Business in Education?," *Harvard Business Review*, March-April 1991, pp. 54 and 62. Data from the Japan Productivity Center are from Joji Arai's article "Productivity Experience in Japan," *International Productivity Journal*, Spring 1990, pp. 59-65.

CHAPTER 6

The facts and figures on infrastructure come from four main sources: David A. Aschauer's article "Public Investment and Private Sector Growth" (Economic Policy Institute, 1990); Aschauer's "Why Is Infrastructure Important?," a paper prepared for the Federal Reserve Bank of Boston, 1991; Heywood T. Sanders' article "Public Works and Public Dollars" (The House Wednesday Group, February 1991); and Carol A. Evans, Kenneth A. Small, and Clifford Winston's, *Road Work* (Brookings, 1989). Aschauer's papers summarize his more technical work on the impact of public infrastructure on productivity. Sanders' paper emphasizes the role of state and local governments and was background for the House Wednesday Group's statement on highway policy, "Rules of the Game" (February 4, 1991). The book by Small et al. is the source of the analysis of efficient highway construction and pricing.

CHAPTER 7

The quotations come from George Gilder's *Wealth and Poverty* (New York: Basic Books, 1981), p. 188; Clyde V. Prestowitz Jr.'s *Trading Places*, p. 14; and Kevin Phillips's *The Politics of Rich and Poor* (New York: Random House, 1990), pp. 220 and 221.

Additional Copies

To order additional copies of *Growing Together*
for friends or colleagues, please write to The Larger
Agenda Series, Whittle Books, 505 Market St.,
Knoxville, Tenn. 37902. For a single copy, please
enclose a check for $11.95 payable to The Larger
Agenda Series. When ordering 10 or more books,
enclose $9.95 for each; for orders of 50 or more,
enclose $7.95 for each. If you wish to order by
phone, call 800-284-1956.

Also available, at the same prices, are copies
of the previous books in The Larger Agenda Series:

The Trouble With Money by William Greider

Adhocracy: The Power to Change
by Robert H. Waterman Jr.

Life After Television by George Gilder

The Book Wars by James Atlas

The X Factor by George Plimpton

A Short History of Financial Euphoria
by John Kenneth Galbraith

Pacific Rift by Michael Lewis

Predicting Russia's Future by Richard Lourie

The Disuniting of America
by Arthur M. Schlesinger Jr.

Please allow two weeks for delivery.
Tennessee residents must add 7¾ percent sales tax.